PREVENTION MAGAZINE'S
QUICK & HEALTHY LOW-FAT COOKING

Healthy Italian Cooking

*From appetizers to desserts, delicious
low-fat dishes inspired by one of the world's
most popular cuisines*

❧ ❧ ❧

Rodale Press, Inc.
Emmaus, Pennsylvania

QUICK AND HEALTHY LOW-FAT COOKING

Managing Editor: JEAN ROGERS
Executive Editor: DEBORA T. YOST
Senior Book Designer: DARLENE SCHNECK
Art Director: JANE COLBY KNUTILA
Associate Art Director: ELIZABETH OTWELL

Healthy Italian Cooking was produced by Rebus, Inc.
Editor: MARYA DALRYMPLE
Recipe Development: MIRIAM RUBIN, MARIANNE ZANZARELLA
Writer: BONNIE J. SLOTNICK
Art Director and Designer: JUDITH HENRY
Production Editor: MICHELE HEARNS

Photographer: ANGELO CAGGIANO
Food Stylists: A. J. BATTIFARANO, DIANE SIMONE VEZZA
Prop Stylist: FRANCINE MATALON-DEGNI
Nutritional Analyses: HILL NUTRITION ASSOCIATES

Library of Congress Cataloging-in-Publication Data

Healthy Italian cooking: from appetizers to desserts, delicious low-fat
    dishes inspired by one of the world's most popular cuisines/edited by
    Jean Rogers, food editor, Prevention Magazine Health Books.
        p.   cm. — (Prevention magazine's quick & healthy low-fat cooking)
    Includes index.
    ISBN 0–87596–326–9   hardcover
    ISBN 0–87596–327–7   paperback
        1. Cookery, Italian.   2. Low-fat diet—Recipes.   I. Rogers, Jean.
II. Series.
    TX723.H4   1996
    641.5945—dc20   96–817

Distributed in the book trade by St. Martin's Press

2   4   6   8   10   9   7   5   3   1   hardcover
2   4   6   8   10   9   7   5   3   1   paperback

CONTENTS

❧ ❧ ❧

Appetizers & Soups   16

For starters, choose a hearty soup or a light one—
or a risotto, vegetables or shrimp

Pasta Dishes   34

Beyond "red sauce"—pasta partnered with pesto,
fennel, arugula, asparagus, beef, turkey
and more

Poultry, Fish & Meat   60

Taste-tempting Italian dishes using chicken and turkey,
sole and salmon, lamb and pork

Side Dishes   86

The greens, grains and other accompaniments
that make an Italian meal complete

Desserts   104

From crisp biscotti and refreshing ices
to decadent—but low-fat—tiramisù and cheesecake

PREFACE

❧ ❧ ❧

There's no doubting the popularity of Italian food on this side of the Atlantic. Surveys of *Prevention*'s faithful readers and cookbook buyers repeatedly confirm that fact. Whenever we ask them what their favorite cuisine is, we can count on Italian scoring at the top. And it's not just pasta that's hot. These days, risotto, polenta, foccacia, pesto, tiramisù, biscotti and sauces with names like arrabbiata and primavera have worked their way onto our tables and into our vocabulary. Still, pasta remains a major component of the Italian meals we enjoy both at home and in restaurants.

Not long ago, weight watchers shunned noodles of all sorts. They mistakenly considered pasta fattening, not realizing that the fault—if any—lay with the sauce and other extras that commonly adorn this food. Heavy meat sauces, cream sauces, egg sauces, cheese sauces and even some innocent-looking but fat-laden tomato sauces were the real culprits. In fact, a filling two-ounce serving of plain pasta contains a modest 200 calories. Topping it with a wealth of vegetables, a dab of olive oil and a sprinkling of cheese does little to mar that svelte profile.

And now that once-exotic ingredients—sun-dried tomatoes, porcini and other mushrooms, lean imported ham, fresh herbs of infinite variety, broccoli rabe, bulb fennel and balsamic vinegar—are common in many supermarkets, cooks can add full-bodied flavor to pasta (and to many other Italian dishes) without submerging them in a sea of calories or fat. Italian food sparkles with flavors previously unfamiliar to Americans.

Indeed, today's Italian cuisine is a far cry from what most of us grew up on. The recipes in this book offer a taste of the new—healthy—Italian table. Enjoy!

Jean Rogers

JEAN ROGERS
Food Editor
Prevention Magazine Health Books

INTRODUCTION

❧ ❧ ❧

America has had a long-standing love affair with Italian food. For generations, Americans of every ethnicity have tucked regularly into plates of spaghetti and meatballs. Lately, we've expanded our repertoire to include the likes of tortellini, linguine, penne, fusilli, radiatore, agnolotti and perciatelli—all collectively known as pasta. Americans now eat pasta in quantities that total more than one billion pounds per year. And while pasta lovers abound, pizza fans are equally numerous. Soldiers returning from service in Italy during World War II formed the first wave of American pizza promoters. Today, pizza is rated America's most popular snack food.

Of course, there's much more to Italian cooking than just pasta and pizza, and the cuisine is as complex as the country itself. Italy was not united as a nation until 1861, and the separate regions have, for the most part, clung to their individual identities, especially where food is concerned. For instance, you'll find the bountiful seafood and vegetable salad called *cappon magro* only in Liguria (which is also the home of *pesto);* and *ribollito,* a hearty vegetable soup, is still a signature dish of Tuscany. Although the love of tomatoes has spread throughout Italy, baked pasta with mozzarella and tomato sauce continues to be strongly identified with Campagna.

While the majority of the 20,000 (and growing) Italian restaurants in the United States serve up tomato-centered southern Italian cuisine, recipes from other areas, particularly Tuscany, are turning up more frequently on menus. The recipes in this book represent a wide selection of dishes from all over Italy, focusing on those that maintain a healthy balance of carbohydrates to protein and fat. Historically, the Italian diet consisted predominantly of grains and grain products (pasta, bread, rice, polenta) and legumes (beans, peas and lentils); a wealth of vegetables; and just

enough meat, poultry, seafood or cheese to flavor the lower-fat components of the meal. As with many ethnic cuisines, however, the balance changed when Italians came to the New World—and now Americans expect every pasta dish they order to come blanketed with cheese and every pizza to be paved with pepperoni.

Here you will find recipes that return to Italy's healthier heritage: There are grain- and legume-based specialties such as Risotto with Asparagus (page 20) and Tuscan White Bean Soup (page 25); and traditional Italian vegetable dishes like Artichokes with Lemon-Chive Dip (page 22) and Baked Baby Eggplant Fans (page 26). You'll be pleased, too, with the wealth of pasta ideas: Ziti with Sausage, Peppers and Onions (page 52) and Tortellini with Creamy Tomato Sauce (page 54) are just two choices. Meat-eaters will be happy with Steak Oreganata with Mushrooms (page 65) or Minted Lamb Chops with White Beans (page 73). And, if you prefer poultry or fish, try Chicken Breasts Arrabbiata (page 62) or Sole Florentine (page 71). Don't worry, you needn't skip dessert: You can treat yourself to a ravishingly rich (but low-fat) Ricotta Cheesecake (page 116) or a luscious layered Tiramisù (page 108).

Not to give short shrift to that universal favorite, the first six pages of the book teach you to make great pizza at home. Your favorite toppings are here, as well as a sophisticated variation: White Pizza with Onions and Rosemary (page 11). You'll also learn to fill and fold calzone—satisfying stuffed pizza "pockets" that make a great casual supper.

Following the section on pizza, on pages 14 and 15, you'll find an informal visual "glossary" of basic Italian ingredients. Thanks to America's passion for Italian food, most of them are available at your local market.

Pizza Variations

Instead of always "ordering in," why not try making pizza at home for a change? It's a fun project for the whole family (hide the mixer and have the kids knead the dough) that allows you to customize your pie as no pizzeria can. Homemade pies are also bound to be lower in fat, and you can pump up the nutrients by piling on extra veggies. Here are pizzas large and small, as well as the pizza pockets called calzone.

BASIC PIZZA DOUGH

❧ ❧ ❧

Making pizza dough is exactly like making bread dough, but rather than letting the dough rise a second time, you press it out in a pan, ready for toppings. Be sure to check the date on the packet of yeast before you use it: Active dry yeast keeps for months (store it in the refrigerator), but like all yeast, it must be alive to do its work of raising the dough.

1½ **teaspoons active dry yeast**

½ **teaspoon sugar**

¾ **cup lukewarm water (105° to 115°)**

1¼ **to 1½ cups unbleached all-purpose flour**

¾ **cup whole-wheat flour**

¼ **teaspoon salt**

1 In a small bowl, sprinkle the yeast and sugar over ¼ cup of the lukewarm water; stir until dissolved. Let stand for 5 to 10 minutes, or until foamy.

2 Meanwhile, in a large bowl (or the bowl of a stationary electric mixer fitted with a paddle), mix 1 cup of the all-purpose flour, the whole-wheat flour and salt. Add the yeast mixture and the remaining ½ cup lukewarm water, and stir (or mix at low speed) until a soft dough forms. If the dough seems to be sticky, add the remaining flour, 1 tablespoon at a time, as needed.

3 If kneading with a mixer, switch to the dough hook after Step 2 and knead the dough for 3 to 4 minutes, or until the dough clings to the dough hook and is smooth and elastic. Otherwise, gather the dough into a ball and knead on a lightly floured surface for about 5 minutes, or until the dough is smooth and elastic and forms blisters when shaped into a ball. While kneading, add additional flour, a little at a time, as needed to keep it from sticking.

4 Spray a medium bowl with no-stick spray. Place the dough in the bowl and turn to coat with the spray. Cover the bowl with plastic wrap and let the dough rise in a warm place for 30 to 45 minutes, or until doubled in bulk.

5 Punch down the dough and continue as directed in the recipes that follow.

Per ¼ crust without topping 249 calories, 1.1 g. fat, 0.5 g. saturated fat, 0 mg. cholesterol, 138 mg. sodium
Makes one 12-inch crust

ZESTY PIZZA SAUCE

❧ ❧ ❧

You could use a bottled pasta or pizza sauce on your pizza (you'll need 1 cup for this recipe), but this quick homemade version makes an especially good pie. Double or triple the recipe, if you like, and freeze it in 1-cup portions.

3 **garlic cloves, crushed**

1 **teaspoon extra-virgin olive oil**

½ **teaspoon sugar**

½ teaspoon dried basil, crumbled

¼ teaspoon fennel seeds

¼ teaspoon dried thyme, crumbled

⅛ teaspoon freshly ground black pepper

⅛ teaspoon crushed red pepper flakes

1 cup canned crushed tomatoes

1 In a medium, heavy no-stick skillet, combine the garlic, oil, sugar, basil, fennel seeds, thyme, black pepper and red pepper flakes. Cook over medium-high heat, stirring constantly, for 1 to 2 minutes, or until the mixture begins to sizzle and is fragrant.

2 Stir in the tomatoes and bring to a boil. Reduce the heat to medium-low and simmer, uncovered, for 10 minutes, or until the sauce thickens.

Per ¼ cup 29 calories, 1.3 g. fat, 0.2 g. saturated fat, 0 mg. cholesterol, 98 mg. sodium **Makes 1 cup**

Two-Tomato and Cheese Pizzettes

❧ ❧ ❧

Delicious as is—topped with sauce, tomatoes, mozzarella and basil—these individual pizzas also present a versatile platform for other tasty toppings. Try steamed, thinly sliced broccoli, blanched spinach, sliced mushrooms or roasted bell peppers.

2 tablespoons cornmeal

1 recipe Basic Pizza Dough (opposite)

1 recipe Zesty Pizza Sauce (opposite and above)

8 medium plum tomatoes, thinly sliced crosswise

¾ cup finely shredded fresh basil leaves

1 garlic clove, crushed

¼ teaspoon salt

¼ teaspoon freshly ground black pepper

4 ounces part-skim mozzarella cheese, shredded

1 Preheat the oven to 450°. Spray 2 baking sheets with no-stick spray and dust each with 1 tablespoon of the cornmeal.

2 Divide the Basic Pizza Dough into 4 equal pieces. Working with 1 piece of dough at a time and keeping the rest covered with plastic wrap or a towel, stretch, pull and pat the dough to make an irregular flattened disk, 7 to 8 inches in diameter. (If you prefer, you can roll out the dough with a floured rolling pin on a floured work surface. Be sure to dust off any excess flour with a pastry brush.) Place 2 of the rounds on each of the prepared baking sheets.

3 Spread one-fourth (about ¼ cup) of the Zesty Pizza Sauce over each dough round, leaving a ½-inch border. Bake both sheets at once for 7 to 10 minutes, or until the crusts are lightly browned on the bottom and the sauce is set. Remove from the oven.

4 While the crusts are baking, in a medium bowl, toss the tomatoes with the basil, garlic, salt and black pepper. Leaving the juices in the bowl, arrange the tomatoes on the sauce, leaving a ¾-inch border. Sprinkle with the mozzarella.

5 Bake for 7 to 8 minutes, or until the tomatoes are warmed, the crusts browned and the cheese melted.

Per serving 395 calories, 8 g. fat, 3.2 g. saturated fat, 16 mg. cholesterol, 512 mg. sodium **Serves 4**

SAUSAGE, MUSHROOM
AND PEPPER PIZZA

❧ ❧ ❧

Italian turkey sausage, which comes in both sweet
and hot styles, makes possible a low-fat sausage pizza.

- 1 tablespoon cornmeal
- 1 recipe Basic Pizza Dough (see page 8)
- 1 recipe Zesty Pizza Sauce (see pages 8–9)
- 6 ounces Italian-style turkey sausage (sweet, hot or a
  combination of the two)
- 1½ teaspoons extra-virgin olive oil
- 8 ounces fresh mushrooms, sliced
- 1 medium red bell pepper, cut into thin strips
- 1 medium green bell pepper, cut into thin strips
- 2 to 3 tablespoons defatted chicken broth
- 2 ounces part-skim mozzarella cheese, shredded

1 Preheat the oven to 500°. Spray a 12-inch round
pizza pan or a large baking sheet with no-stick spray.
Sprinkle with the cornmeal.

2 On a lightly floured surface, with a floured rolling
pin, roll out the Basic Pizza Dough to a 13-inch circle.
With a pastry brush, remove any excess flour. Transfer
the dough to the prepared pan. (If using a pizza pan,
press the dough up the sides; if using a baking sheet,
roll and pinch the edge of the dough into a raised
border.)

3 Spread the sauce over the dough and bake for 6
to 10 minutes (depending on how crisp you like your
crust), or until the crust is lightly browned and the
sauce is hot. Remove the crust from the oven.

4 While the crust is baking, remove the sausage from
its casings and crumble the sausage into a large, heavy
no-stick skillet. Place the skillet over medium heat
and cook, stirring to break up the chunks, for 5 to 6
minutes, or until the sausage is lightly browned and
cooked through. Drain the sausage on paper towels.

5 In the same skillet, warm the oil over medium-
high heat. Add the mushrooms and bell peppers, and
sauté for 2 minutes, or until the mushrooms start to
brown. Drizzle with 2 tablespoons of the broth,
reduce the heat to medium and sauté for 4 to 6 minutes longer, or until the vegetables are tender (add 1
more tablespoon broth if the pan seems dry).

6 Scatter the vegetables evenly over the crust and sprinkle with the sausage and cheese. Bake for another 10 minutes, or until the cheese is melted, the vegetables warmed and the crust golden brown.

Per serving 441 calories, 11.7 g. fat, 3.3 g. saturated fat, 31 mg. cholesterol, 623 mg. sodium **Serves 4**

WHITE PIZZA WITH ONIONS AND ROSEMARY

❧ ❧ ❧

Dried rosemary will need to cook longer than fresh; add it to the skillet along with the onions.

- 1 **tablespoon cornmeal**
- 1 **teaspoon extra-virgin olive oil**
- 5 **cups thinly sliced onions**
- 6 **garlic cloves, slivered**
- ¾ **teaspoon sugar**
- ¼ **teaspoon salt**
- ¼ **teaspoon freshly ground black pepper, or more to taste**
- ¼ **cup defatted chicken broth**
- 1½ **teaspoons chopped fresh rosemary or ½ teaspoon dried rosemary**
- 1 **recipe Basic Pizza Dough (see page 8)**
- 4 **ounces part-skim mozzarella cheese, shredded**
- 2 **ounces Parmesan cheese, grated**
- ⅛ **teaspoon crushed red pepper flakes**

    Fresh rosemary sprigs, for garnish (optional)

1 Preheat the oven to 500°. Spray a 12-inch round pizza pan or a large baking sheet with no-stick spray. Sprinkle with the cornmeal.

2 In a large, heavy no-stick skillet, warm the oil over medium-high heat until hot but not smoking. Add the onions, garlic, sugar, salt and black pepper, and sauté for 6 to 7 minutes, or until the onions begin to brown. Reduce the heat to medium, drizzle the onions with 1 tablespoon of the broth and cook, stirring frequently and adding the remaining broth, 1 tablespoon at a time, for 8 to 10 minutes longer, or until the onions are very tender. Sprinkle with the rosemary.

3 Meanwhile, on a lightly floured surface, with a floured rolling pin, roll out the Basic Pizza Dough to a 13-inch circle. With a pastry brush, remove any excess flour. Transfer the dough to the prepared pan. (If using a pizza pan, press the dough up the sides; if using a baking sheet, roll and pinch the edge of the dough into a raised border.)

4 Spread the onions evenly over the crust. Bake for 8 to 10 minutes, or until the crust begins to brown.

5 Sprinkle the mozzarella, Parmesan and red pepper flakes over the onions. Bake for 8 to 10 minutes longer, or until the cheeses melt and the crust is lightly browned. Garnish with rosemary sprigs, if desired.

Per serving 501 calories, 11.9 g. fat, 5.9 g. saturated fat, 28 mg. cholesterol, 738 mg. sodium **Serves 4**

HERBED CHICKEN CALZONES

❧ ❧ ❧

These pizza turnovers are stuffed with a tempting mixture of chicken, ricotta and mozzarella.

- 2 tablespoons cornmeal
- 4 ounces skinless, boneless chicken breast, cut into chunks
- 1 teaspoon extra-virgin olive oil
- ½ cup diced bottled roasted red peppers, rinsed and drained
- 2 tablespoons chopped scallion
- ¼ teaspoon salt
- ¼ teaspoon freshly ground black pepper
- ⅔ cup part-skim ricotta cheese
- ½ cup nonfat ricotta cheese
- 2 ounces part-skim mozzarella cheese, shredded
- 1 tablespoon chopped Italian parsley
- 1½ teaspoons chopped fresh thyme
- 1 recipe Basic Pizza Dough (see page 8)

1 Preheat the oven to 450°. Dust 2 baking sheets with 1 tablespoon cornmeal each.

2 Place the chicken in a food processor and pulse until ground medium-fine.

3 In a medium, heavy no-stick skillet, warm the oil over medium-high heat until hot but not smoking.

1 Roll out each of the flattened disks of dough to a 7-inch circle; brush off any excess flour.

2 Using a ½-cup measure for each portion, divide the filling among the rounds of dough.

3 Moisten the edges of the dough, then fold the dough over the filling and press the edges firmly together.

4 Starting from one end, roll the edge over itself and crimp together to seal.

Crumble in the chicken. Add the roasted red peppers, scallions, salt and black pepper, and stir to combine. Cook, stirring and breaking up the chunks of chicken, for 2 to 3 minutes, or until the chicken is cooked through. Transfer to a medium bowl.

4 Add the part-skim and nonfat ricotta cheeses, the mozzarella, parsley and thyme to the chicken, and stir to combine.

5 Divide the dough into 4 equal pieces. Shape each piece of dough into a flattened disk. On a lightly floured surface, with a floured rolling pin, roll out each piece of dough to a 7-inch circle. With a pastry brush, brush off any excess flour.

6 Spoon ½ cup of the filling onto each circle, leaving a 1-inch border. Moisten the edge of the dough around the filling with a finger that has been dipped in cold water. Fold the dough over the filling and press the edges together to seal them. Gently press the filling inside the dough into any pockets in the dough. Roll the edges over themselves to make a rolled border.

7 With a large spatula, transfer the filled calzones to the prepared baking sheets, placing 2 calzones on each of the baking sheets.

8 Bake the calzones, switching the pans on the racks halfway through baking so the calzones cook evenly, for 17 to 20 minutes, or until the dough is well browned and crisp.

Per serving 431 calories, 8.2 g. fat, 3.9 g. saturated fat, 37 mg. cholesterol, 481 mg. sodium **Serves 4**

ITALIAN INGREDIENTS

Slender white *cannellini* (at right) are but one of the many varieties of beans beloved by Italians. Beans cooked from scratch are best, but rinsed, drained canned beans are fine for most recipes.

Meaty, flavorful fresh tomatoes are required for some Italian dishes, but when they're not available, use canned or sun-dried tomatoes as stand-ins and flavor boosters. Dried mushrooms—imported porcini are shown below—are a potent seasoning for soups and sauces.

Peppery arugula leaves give any salad authentic Italian flair; try them sautéed, too.

Fresh sage, rosemary and oregano (above) are prized in the Italian kitchen. Sage is a favorite in the northern part of the country, while oregano is grown and used mostly in the south; rosemary is widely popular.

It's well worth seeking out fresh herbs—or growing them yourself, which you can easily do if you have a sunny windowsill. Dried herbs differ somewhat in taste from their fresh counterparts, but—fortunately—sage, rosemary and oregano retain their flavor better than most dried herbs.

It's easy to make an Italian meal at a moment's notice if you always keep pasta on hand. Fill your cupboards and freezer with an assortment of dried and fresh pastas—there are hundreds of varieties to choose from. Filled pastas, such as the ravioli and tortellini shown here, are almost a meal in themselves. Dried pastas vary in quality: Try a few different brands until you find one that regularly cooks to a perfect al dente consistency—and never overcook it.

Italian dishes don't
require large quantities
of cheese; a few spoonfuls of
grated or crumbled cheese can supply
the needed accent. So insist on superb quality: Buy *Parmigiano-Reggiano*—authentic Italian Parmesan—and grate it yourself in small amounts. For a change, try *asiago*, which is milder, or the more robust *pecorino romano*. Seek out a good cheese shop (look for the sign *"latticini freschi"* in an Italian neighborhood) where you can buy excellent gorgonzola and fresh mozzarella.

Italians prefer plump, pearly Arborio rice for risotto because its starchy exterior cooks into a creamy sauce while the heart of the grain remains firm.

Two other irreplaceable Italian imports are extra-virgin olive oil and balsamic vinegar. Since you won't need a lot of oil for the recipes in this book, it's worth the extra cost to buy the finest.

Balsamic vinegar, made from grape juice rather than wine and aged in wooden casks, is uniquely sweet and mild.

Appetizers
& Soups

❧ ❧ ❧

FOR STARTERS, CHOOSE A

HEARTY SOUP OR A LIGHT ONE—

OR A RISOTTO, VEGETABLES

OR SHRIMP

QUICK TOMATO AND BREAD SOUP

2 cups water

⅓ cup sun-dried tomatoes (not oil-packed)

2 teaspoons extra-virgin olive oil

1 cup chopped onions

3 garlic cloves, minced, plus 1 garlic clove, peeled and halved

1 can (16 ounces) crushed tomatoes in purée

1 can (8 ounces) no-salt-added tomato sauce

¼ teaspoon sugar

¼ teaspoon freshly ground black pepper

⅛ teaspoon salt

⅛ teaspoon crushed red pepper flakes

8 slices (¼-ounce each) crusty Italian bread

½ cup chopped fresh basil

Whole basil leaves, for garnish (optional)

Kitchen shears—an essential for any efficient cook—are perfect for snipping dried tomatoes.

Preceding pages: Minestrone Verde (recipe on page 29)

Canned tomato soup has a few points in its favor: It is cheap, quick and easy to prepare. On the other hand, it also has an excessively salty, undeniably "tinny" taste and a dismayingly high sodium content. So put away your can opener and fix this thick, garlicky triple-tomato soup instead. Ladle the soup over a couple of crusty Italian-bread toasts and prepare for a treat.

1 In a small saucepan, bring 1 cup of the water to a boil over high heat. Remove the pan from the heat, stir in the sun-dried tomatoes, cover and let stand for 8 to 10 minutes, or until the tomatoes are softened. Reserving ¼ cup of the soaking liquid, drain the tomatoes, then cut them into small pieces with kitchen shears or chop with a knife.

2 Preheat the broiler.

3 In a medium no-stick saucepan, warm the oil over medium heat until hot but not smoking. Add the onions and minced garlic, and sauté for 4 to 5 minutes, or until tender.

4 Add the remaining 1 cup water, the crushed tomatoes, tomato sauce, sugar, black pepper, salt and red pepper flakes to the onion mixture. Add the sun-dried tomatoes and the reserved soaking liquid, and stir to combine. Increase the heat to high and bring to a boil. Reduce the heat to medium-low, cover and simmer for 10 minutes to blend the flavors.

5 Meanwhile, arrange the bread on a baking sheet. Toast under the broiler 4 to 5 inches from the heat for about 1 minute per side, or until lightly browned. Rub one side of each slice with the halved garlic clove.

6 Remove the soup from the heat and stir in the chopped basil. Divide the soup among 4 soup plates and top each serving with 2 slices of the toasted bread. Garnish with whole basil leaves, if desired.

***

Preparation time 15 minutes • **Total time** 40 minutes • **Per serving** 155 calories, 3.2 g. fat (19% of calories), 0.5 g. saturated fat, 0 mg. cholesterol, 353 mg. sodium, 3.3 g. dietary fiber, 113 mg. calcium, 2 mg. iron, 32 mg. vitamin C, 1 mg. beta-carotene • **Serves 4**

***

RISOTTO WITH ASPARAGUS

3¼ cups water

¾ cup defatted chicken broth

8 ounces fresh asparagus spears, trimmed and cut diagonally into 1-inch pieces

½ cup grated carrots

¾ cup Arborio rice

1 teaspoon extra-virgin olive oil

1 tablespoon grated Parmesan cheese

1 tablespoon chopped Italian parsley

⅛ teaspoon salt

⅛ teaspoon freshly ground black pepper, or more to taste

Risotto is often served as a first course in Italy; and even a little "tasting" portion of this dish is flavorful. The rice is prepared quite differently from the standard American method: Rather than cooking it in a covered pot of boiling water, you add hot liquid a little at a time, stirring all the while. Stop adding the broth when the rice is just al dente; don't worry if a little broth is left over.

1 In a medium saucepan, combine the water and broth. Cover and bring to a boil over high heat. Add the asparagus, return to a boil and cook, uncovered, for 2 to 3 minutes, or until crisp-tender. Add the carrots and cook for 2 to 3 seconds longer. Remove the asparagus and carrots from the liquid with a small strainer. Cool the vegetables under cold running water and set aside. Reduce the heat under the broth mixture so it is just simmering.

2 In a medium, heavy saucepan, combine the rice and oil. Place the pan over medium-high heat and cook, stirring frequently, for 2 to 3 minutes, or until some of the grains of rice turn golden.

3 Reduce the heat under the rice to medium. Add a big ladleful of the broth mixture to the rice and bring to a boil. Cook, stirring frequently, for 1 to 3 minutes, or until the liquid is nearly absorbed. Repeat the process with most of the remaining broth mixture, adding a ladleful at a time, until the rice is creamy and al dente, and the liquid is nearly absorbed (this will take about 15 minutes).

4 Stir the asparagus and carrots into the rice, and cook for 1 to 2 minutes, or just until heated through. Remove the pan from the heat and stir in the Parmesan, parsley, salt and black pepper.

Preparation time 10 minutes • **Total time** 40 minutes • **Per serving** 172 calories, 2.2 g. fat (12% of calories), 0.5 g. saturated fat, 1 mg. cholesterol, 286 mg. sodium, 1.3 g. dietary fiber, 34 mg. calcium, 2 mg. iron, 17 mg. vitamin C, 2.6 mg. beta-carotene • **Serves 4**

MARKET AND PANTRY
The traditional rice for risotto is short-grained, starchy Italian Arborio, which, when cooked, turns creamy on the out-side while remaining al dente within. Arborio is the generic name; you'll find the rice sold under various brand names in Italian markets and gourmet shops.

ARTICHOKES WITH LEMON-CHIVE DIP

1 large onion, cut into thick slices

⅓ cup fresh lemon juice

2 unpeeled garlic cloves, smashed

¾ teaspoon freshly ground black pepper

4 medium artichokes (about 10 ounces each)

1 large shallot

¼ cup low-fat mayonnaise

¼ cup nonfat sour cream

2 tablespoons snipped fresh chives

¼ teaspoon dried mint, crumbled

Whole chives, for garnish (optional)

The rich soil of the area around Rome—the region known as Lazio—produces a number of varieties of artichokes: purple or yellow, round or elongated. These splendid vegetables are grilled, braised, deep fried or, when young and tender, even eaten raw. Here the artichokes are cooked in a lightly flavored lemon-garlic "broth," then served with a creamy herbed sauce.

1 Fill a large pot with water. Add the onions, 2 tablespoons of the lemon juice, the garlic and ½ teaspoon of the black pepper. Cover and bring to a boil over high heat. Reduce the heat to medium and simmer for 5 minutes to blend the flavors.

2 Meanwhile, rinse the artichokes and trim the stems flat. Using a stainless-steel knife or kitchen shears, cut off the ends of the leaves.

3 Add the artichokes to the pot, increase the heat to high and bring to a boil. Reduce the heat to medium, cover and simmer for 20 to 30 minutes, or until the stems of the artichokes are tender when pierced with a fork. Transfer the artichokes to 4 soup plates.

4 While the artichokes are cooking, make the dipping sauce. Peel and finely mince the shallot. Place the minced shallots in a small bowl. Add the mayonnaise, sour cream, chives, mint and the remaining lemon juice and ¼ teaspoon black pepper. Whisk to blend well.

5 Garnish the artichokes with whole chives, if desired. Serve with the dipping sauce on the side.

Snip or cut off the ends of the artichoke leaves, which are tipped with thornlike points. Use a stainless-steel knife or shears: Carbon steel will cause the artichokes to discolor.

Preparation time 10 minutes • **Total time** 45 minutes • **Per serving** 121 calories, 1.3 g. fat (9% of calories), 0.1 g. saturated fat, 0 mg. cholesterol, 259 mg. sodium, 7 g. dietary fiber, 88 mg. calcium, 2 mg. iron, 28 mg. vitamin C, 0.2 mg. beta-carotene
Serves 4

FOODWAYS

If you've never eaten an artichoke, you may need some help in dealing with this somewhat daunting delicacy. To begin, pull off a leaf, dip it into the sauce and put the base of the leaf in your mouth; pull it out between your closed teeth to scrape off the fleshy part. When you've finished the leaves, use a knife or spoon to scrape off the fuzzy top of the artichoke heart (it looks like the center of a daisy). Then cut the heart into pieces and eat it.

TUSCAN WHITE BEAN SOUP

2 teaspoons extra-virgin olive oil

1 cup diced carrots

1 cup sliced celery

1 cup diced onions

2 garlic cloves, minced

2 teaspoons chopped fresh rosemary or ½ teaspoon dried rosemary

¼ teaspoon salt

¼ teaspoon freshly ground black pepper

¾ cup defatted chicken broth

1 can (19 ounces) cannellini beans, rinsed and drained

2 cups water

8 ounces baking potato, peeled and diced (1¼ cups)

Fresh rosemary sprigs, for garnish (optional)

Chicken soup's reputation as the ultimate comfort food is hard to challenge, but this Italian classic is a strong contender for the title. The vegetables are cooked and some are reserved for a topping; then the rest are gently mashed, leaving the soup slightly chunky. The flavors, too, are ever-so-soothing: Even the garlic is sweet and mild after simmering for 15 to 20 minutes.

1 In a large no-stick saucepan, warm the oil over medium heat. Stir in the carrots, celery, onions, garlic, rosemary, salt and black pepper. Sauté for 2 minutes, or until the vegetables begin to soften.

2 Drizzle the vegetables with 2 tablespoons of the broth, reduce the heat to medium-low, cover and cook, stirring occasionally, for 8 to 10 minutes, or until the vegetables are very tender. Scoop out ¾ cup of the vegetables and place in a small bowl. Cover with plastic wrap to keep warm; set aside.

3 Add the beans, water and potatoes to the pan. Increase the heat to high, cover and bring to a boil. Reduce the heat to medium and simmer, covered, for 8 minutes, or until the potatoes are tender.

4 Remove the pan from the heat and, using a potato masher or whisk, mash the soup to a chunky texture. Ladle the soup into 4 bowls, then spoon some of the reserved vegetables on top of each serving. Garnish with a rosemary sprig, if desired.

Preparation time 15 minutes • **Total time** 45 minutes • **Per serving** 189 calories, 3.7 g. fat (17% of calories), 0.4 g. saturated fat, 0 mg. cholesterol, 530 mg. sodium, 8.1 g. dietary fiber, 66 mg. calcium, 2 mg. iron, 17 mg. vitamin C, 4.7 mg. beta-carotene • **Serves 4**

❧ ❧ ❧

ON THE MENU
For a hearty supper on a cold evening, serve an Italian version of the soup-and-sandwich meal. Accompany the bean soup with slabs of *focaccia*—a thick yeast bread often flavored with rosemary or sage—and a selection of roasted vegetables as sandwich fillings. You might offer multicolored bell peppers, eggplant, tomatoes and onions. Just cut the vegetables thin, brush them very lightly with olive oil and broil until lightly charred.

BAKED BABY EGGPLANT FANS

4 **baby eggplants (each about 4 ounces)**

3 **garlic cloves, crushed**

2 **teaspoons chopped fresh thyme or ½ teaspoon dried thyme**

¼ **teaspoon salt**

¼ **teaspoon freshly ground black pepper**

4 **large plum tomatoes, cut lengthwise into ¼-inch-thick slices**

1 **large onion, halved lengthwise, each half cut into six ¼-inch-thick slices**

1 **ounce part-skim mozzarella cheese, shredded**

½ **cup defatted chicken broth**

Fresh thyme sprigs, for garnish (optional)

After the fashion of a classic Sicilian recipe, the eggplants in this first course are cut into slices, which are left attached at the top, then fanned out. In Sicily, the fanned eggplants are deep-fried; for this prettier, more healthful dish, tomatoes, onions and mozzarella are interleaved with the eggplants before the fans are baked.

1 Preheat the oven to 450°.

2 Wash and dry the eggplants; do not trim the stem ends. Make 7 lengthwise slices in each eggplant, cutting through the blossom end, but leaving the stem end intact so the slices remain attached. Flatten the eggplants with the heel of your hand so the slices fan out.

3 In a cup, combine the garlic, thyme, salt and black pepper. With your fingers, rub a little of the garlic mixture onto the cut sides of the eggplant slices.

4 Alternately fill the eggplant fans with the tomato and onion slices, using 4 slices of tomato and 3 slices of onion for each eggplant. Press a little of the cheese into each filled slice. Arrange the eggplant fans in a single layer in a 13 x 9-inch baking pan.

5 Pour the broth into the pan, then cover the pan with foil. Bake the eggplants for 30 minutes. Uncover and bake for 5 minutes longer, or until the eggplants are very tender.

6 Transfer the eggplant fans to a platter; discard the broth left in the pan. Garnish each fan with thyme sprigs, if desired.

Slice the eggplants from the blossom end, up to but not through the stem end.

Preparation time 10 minutes • **Total time** 1 hour • **Per serving** 86 calories, 1.6 g. fat (17% of calories), 0.8 g. saturated fat, 4 mg. cholesterol, 242 mg. sodium, 3.3 g. dietary fiber, 109 mg. calcium, 1 mg. iron, 16 mg. vitamin C, 0.3 mg. beta-carotene • **Serves 4**

SUBSTITUTION

If you can't get baby eggplants, use one large eggplant for two servings. Cut the eggplant in half lengthwise, place the halves cut-side down and slice into fans.

KITCHEN TIP

After filling the eggplant fans with tomatoes, onions and cheese, use a wide metal spatula—or two, if necessary—to transfer the fans to the baking pan.

MINESTRONE VERDE

2 teaspoons extra-virgin olive oil

1 small leek, white and green parts, halved lengthwise, rinsed of grit and thinly sliced

1 large celery stalk with leaves, thinly sliced

2 garlic cloves, minced, plus 1 whole garlic clove, peeled

¼ teaspoon dried oregano, crumbled

¼ teaspoon freshly ground black pepper

⅛ teaspoon salt

2 cups water

2 cups cut-up Swiss chard (1-inch pieces)

1 cup defatted chicken broth

⅔ cup frozen baby lima beans

¼ cup ditalini or other small pasta

¼ cup Italian parsley sprigs

½ cup frozen green peas

1 tablespoon plus 1 teaspoon shredded Parmesan cheese

As a change from multicolored minestrones, this version has an all-green color scheme, featuring leeks, Swiss chard, lima beans, peas and parsley. In a welcome departure from tradition, the soup simmers for only about 15 minutes rather than the 2 to 3 hours an old-fashioned minestrone would require.

1 In a large flameproof casserole or heavy no-stick saucepan, warm the oil over medium heat until hot but not smoking. Stir in the leeks, celery, minced garlic cloves, oregano, black pepper and salt. Sauté for 3 to 4 minutes, or until the vegetables begin to soften.

2 Stir in the water, Swiss chard, broth, lima beans and pasta. Increase the heat to high, cover and bring to a boil. Reduce the heat to medium-low and simmer, covered, for 8 to 9 minutes, or until the vegetables are tender and the pasta is al dente.

3 Meanwhile, coarsely chop the remaining garlic clove, then mince it together with the parsley.

4 Stir the garlic-parsley mixture and the peas into the soup. Cover and cook for 5 minutes longer, or until the peas are heated through.

5 Ladle the soup into 4 bowls and top each with 1 teaspoon of the Parmesan.

Preparation time 20 minutes • **Total time** 45 minutes • **Per serving** 131 calories, 3.7 g. fat (25% of calories), 0.7 g. saturated fat, 1 mg. cholesterol, 440 mg. sodium, 2.7 g. dietary fiber, 74 mg. calcium, 2 mg. iron, 19 mg. vitamin C, 0.6 mg. beta-carotene • **Serves 4**

MARKET AND PANTRY
Leeks are most plentiful (and cheapest) in the fall and early winter. Small leeks are likely to be the tenderest and sweetest, while very large ones are apt to be woody. To wash leeks, cut off the root ends and the very tops of the leaves, then split the leeks lengthwise. Rinse them well under cold running water, fanning the layers as you do so. In addition to using them in soups, leeks can be braised in broth to serve as a vegetable side dish.

GRILLED SHRIMP AND PEPPER SKEWERS

½ cup packed parsley sprigs

3 tablespoons fresh lemon juice

1 teaspoon extra-virgin olive oil

⅛ teaspoon crushed red pepper flakes

⅛ teaspoon fennel seeds

⅛ teaspoon salt

2 large garlic cloves, peeled

1 large red bell pepper

1 large yellow bell pepper

1 large green bell pepper

Half a large onion

12 medium shrimp, peeled and deveined, with tails attached

4 lemon slices, halved

Eight 6- to 8-inch metal skewers

Parsley sprigs, for garnish (optional)

These *spiedini*—little skewers—of shrimp and vegetables are just the thing to start off a casual party. If you are grilling the skewers (rather than broiling them in the oven), a flat grilling basket that holds the kebabs will make the job easier.

1 Prepare the grill or preheat the broiler and broiler-pan rack.

2 To make the marinade, in a food processor, combine the parsley, lemon juice, oil, red pepper flakes, fennel seeds and salt. With the machine running, drop the garlic through the feed tube; process until finely chopped. Pour the marinade into a medium bowl.

3 Halve and seed all of the bell peppers and cut each into eight 1½-inch pieces. Place the onion half cut-side down and cut lengthwise into 3 wedges. Cut each wedge in half crosswise and separate the layers so you have 20 pieces. Add the bell peppers, onions and shrimp to the marinade, and toss to coat. Cover and let marinate for 5 minutes.

4 Thread 3 shrimp and 2 lemon slices onto 4 of the skewers. On the 4 remaining skewers, alternate different colors of peppers with onion slices, using 6 pieces of pepper (2 of each color) and 5 pieces of onion for each skewer.

5 Place the vegetable skewers on the grill or rack and pour half the marinade from the bowl over the vegetables. Grill or broil 3 to 4 inches from the heat for 3 minutes. Turn the vegetable skewers over.

6 Add the shrimp skewers to the grill or rack with the vegetable skewers and pour the remaining marinade over the shrimp. Grill or broil for 2 to 3 minutes longer, or until the shrimp are pink and cooked through, and the vegetables are tender and lightly charred.

7 Transfer the skewers to a platter. Garnish with parsley sprigs, if desired.

Preparation time 10 minutes • **Total time** 45 minutes • **Per serving** 80 calories, 1.8 g. fat (20% of calories), 0.2 g. saturated fat, 36 mg. cholesterol, 114 mg. sodium, 2.3 g. dietary fiber, 58 mg. calcium, 2 mg. iron, 124 mg. vitamin C, 1.5 mg. beta-carotene • **Serves 4**

ESCAROLE IN BRODO

3 garlic cloves, crushed

1 teaspoon extra-virgin olive oil

½ teaspoon freshly ground
 black pepper

½ teaspoon dried thyme, crumbled

4 cups torn escarole, rinsed

1¾ cups water

1 can (10½ ounces) chick-peas,
 rinsed and drained

¾ cup defatted chicken broth

¾ cup diced plum tomatoes

½ teaspoon sugar

¼ teaspoon salt

¼ cup finely shredded fresh basil

2 teaspoons shredded Parmesan
 cheese

Greens and beans (chick-peas, in this case) served *in brodo*—in broth—make a fine first course. Raw escarole can be quite bitter, but sautéing and then simmering it reduces the assertive flavor to just a pleasant "edge." Be sure to serve the soup with something crisp, such as breadsticks, garlic toasts or flatbread, on the side.

1 In a large no-stick saucepan, combine the garlic, oil, black pepper and thyme. Sauté over medium heat for 1 to 2 minutes, or until the garlic and herbs are fragrant.

2 Add the escarole all at once and increase the heat to high. Cook, stirring frequently, for 1 to 2 minutes, or until the escarole starts to wilt.

3 Stir in the water, chick-peas, broth, tomatoes, sugar and salt, and bring to a boil. Reduce the heat to medium-low, cover and simmer for 5 minutes to blend the flavors.

4 Remove the soup from the heat and stir in the basil. Ladle the soup into 4 bowls and top each serving with ½ teaspoon of the Parmesan.

Preparation time 15 minutes • **Total time** 30 minutes • **Per serving** 95 calories, 3.2 g. fat (30% of calories), 0.4 g. saturated fat, 1 mg. cholesterol, 435 mg. sodium, 3.6 g. dietary fiber, 87 mg. calcium, 2 mg. iron, 11 mg. vitamin C, 0.8 mg. beta-carotene • **Serves 4**

This self-cleaning garlic press produces the equivalent of finely chopped garlic.

Flip the handle over and a set of plastic teeth push out any remaining garlic.

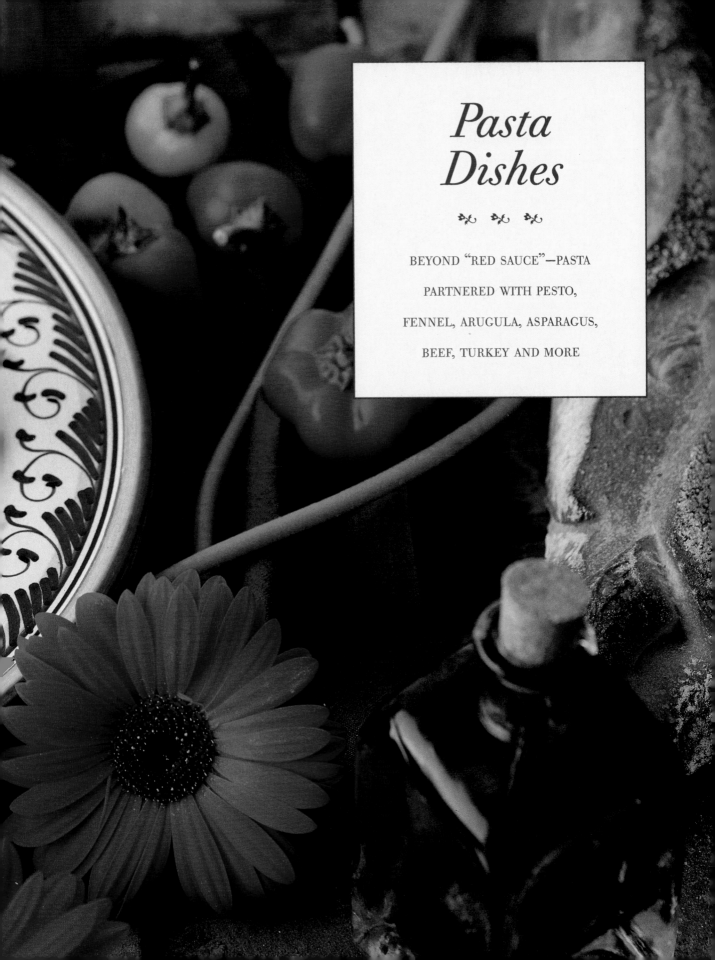

Pasta Dishes

✣ ✣ ✣

BEYOND "RED SAUCE"—PASTA

PARTNERED WITH PESTO,

FENNEL, ARUGULA, ASPARAGUS,

BEEF, TURKEY AND MORE

PASTA WITH GARDEN VEGETABLE SAUCE

1 tablespoon olive oil

6 ounces fresh mushrooms, sliced

2½ cups defatted reduced-sodium chicken broth

¼ cup no-salt-added tomato paste

8 ounces long fusilli or perciatelli

3 cups broccoli florets

2 large carrots, cut in half lengthwise and thinly sliced

1 pound fresh spinach

2 tablespoons minced Italian parsley

1 teaspoon grated lemon zest

1 large garlic clove, minced

¼ teaspoon salt

Lemon zest, for garnish (optional)

Intended for hard-cooked eggs, this wire slicer works beautifully on large mushrooms, too.

If you had a flourishing kitchen garden you might create a sauce similar to this on the spur of the moment. On another day, with different vegetables at their peak, you might make the sauce with cauliflower, green beans and Swiss chard instead. Whether you're "shopping" in your garden or at the market, be flexible when you fix country-style dishes like this one: Feel free to go with the best of what's available rather than slavishly following the recipe.

1 Bring a large covered pot of water to a boil over high heat.

2 In large no-stick skillet, warm the oil over medium heat. Add the mushrooms and cook, stirring occasionally, for 3 to 5 minutes, or until the mushrooms are tender.

3 Add the broth and tomato paste, increase the heat to high and bring to a boil. Reduce the heat to medium and simmer, stirring occasionally, for 6 to 8 minutes, or until the sauce thickens slightly. Remove the skillet from the heat and cover to keep warm.

4 While the sauce is cooking, add the pasta to the boiling water, return to a boil and cook for 9 minutes. Add the broccoli florets and carrots to the pasta water, and continue to cook for 2 to 3 minutes, or until the vegetables are tender and the pasta is al dente.

5 While the sauce and pasta are cooking, wash the spinach well and remove the tough stems. Measure enough spinach to make 2 cups of loosely packed leaves. Coarsely chop the leaves.

6 Add the spinach to the thickened tomato sauce and stir until wilted.

7 Drain the pasta, broccoli and carrots in a colander, then transfer to a large bowl. Pour the sauce over the pasta mixture. Add the parsley, lemon zest, garlic and salt, and toss to combine. Garnish each serving with lemon zest, if desired.

Preparation time 20 minutes • **Total time** 35 minutes • **Per serving** 347 calories, 5.2 g. fat (13% of calories), 0.7 g. saturated fat, 0 mg. cholesterol, 660 mg. sodium, 9.8 g. dietary fiber, 160 mg. calcium, 7 mg. iron, 109 mg. vitamin C, 13 mg. beta-carotene • **Serves 4**

Preceding pages: Ziti with Sausage, Peppers and Onions (recipe on page 52).

PASTA WITH WHITE BEANS AND BACON

8 **ounces cavatelli pasta**

2 **teaspoons olive oil**

2 **large garlic cloves, minced**

2 **ounces trimmed Canadian bacon, diced**

4 **cups cherry or pear tomatoes, stemmed and halved**

1 **can (10½ ounces) cannellini beans, rinsed and drained**

1 **teaspoon fresh rosemary, minced, or ¼ teaspoon dried rosemary, crumbled**

¼ **teaspoon salt**

1 **ounce Parmesan cheese, grated**

Fresh rosemary sprigs, for garnish (optional)

There's something very satisfying about the combination of pasta and beans. It has a richness that requires little adornment in the way of a sauce. Here, it's just the smoky sharpness of Canadian bacon, along with garlic, rosemary and a little Parmesan, that supplies a counterpoint for the *cavatelli* and *cannellini*.

1 Bring a large covered pot of water to a boil over high heat.

2 Add the pasta to the boiling water, return to a boil and cook for 10 to 12 minutes, or according to package directions until al dente.

3 While the pasta is cooking, in a medium no-stick skillet, warm the oil over medium heat. Add the garlic and Canadian bacon, and cook, stirring frequently, for 1 minute, or until the garlic turns golden.

4 Increase the heat to medium-high. Add the cherry or pear tomatoes, the beans, rosemary and salt, and cook for 3 to 5 minutes, or until the tomatoes soften.

5 Drain the pasta in a colander and transfer to a large bowl. Pour the sauce over the pasta, add the Parmesan and toss to combine. Garnish each serving with a rosemary sprig, if desired.

Preparation time 10 minutes • **Total time** 30 minutes • **Per serving** 362 calories, 7 g. fat (17% of calories), 2.2 g. saturated fat, 13 mg. cholesterol, 573 mg. sodium, 5.7 g. dietary fiber, 136 mg. calcium, 4 mg. iron, 24 mg. vitamin C, 0.4 mg. beta-carotene • **Serves 4**

❧ ❧ ❧

One possible substitute for the *cavatelli* is tightly furled *radiatore* pasta.

Another good option is *cavatappi*—hollow, ridged "corkscrews."

PASTA AND CHICKEN WITH TOMATO PESTO

1 cup defatted reduced-sodium
   chicken broth

½ cup sun-dried tomatoes (not oil-
   packed), quartered

12 ounces skinless, boneless
   chicken breast halves

8 ounces radiatore or short fusilli

½ cup loosely packed Italian
   parsley leaves

2 tablespoons balsamic vinegar

1 tablespoon packed fresh thyme
   or ½ teaspoon dried thyme

2 large garlic cloves

1 shallot, quartered

¼ teaspoon freshly ground
   black pepper

8 kalamata olives, pitted and
   chopped

   Fresh thyme sprigs, for garnish
   (optional)

Happily, the food processor has taken the place of the mortar and pestle in the preparation of pesto. In just a few seconds, the machine reduces sun-dried tomatoes, shallots and garlic to a coarse purée. Although the pasta traditionally served with pesto is *trenette* (wide, flat strands), the chicken chunks in this recipe call for a smaller "chunkier" pasta, such as *radiatore*.

1 Preheat the broiler. Spray the broiler-pan rack with no-stick spray. Bring a large covered pot of water to a boil over high heat.

2 In a small saucepan, bring the broth to a boil over high heat. Stir in the sun-dried tomatoes and remove the pan from the heat; let stand for 15 minutes, or until the tomatoes soften.

3 While the sun-dried tomatoes are soaking, place the chicken on the prepared broiler-pan rack and broil 3 to 4 inches from the heat, turning once, for 10 to 12 minutes, or until the chicken is cooked through.

4 While the chicken is cooking, add the pasta to the boiling water, return to a boil and cook for 10 to 12 minutes, or according to package directions until al dente. Drain the pasta in a colander and transfer to a large bowl.

5 While the chicken and pasta are cooking, place the parsley, vinegar, thyme, garlic, shallots and black pepper in a food processor. Add the sun-dried tomatoes and broth, and process until finely chopped.

6 Transfer the chicken to a cutting board and allow to cool slightly. When the chicken has cooled, cut it into ½-inch cubes.

7 Pour the pesto over the pasta. Add the chicken and olives, and toss to combine. Garnish each serving with thyme sprigs, if desired.

Preparation time 20 minutes • **Total time** 40 minutes • **Per serving** 378 calories, 4.6 g. fat (11% of calories), 0.7 g. saturated fat, 49 mg. cholesterol, 416 mg. sodium, 3.9 g. dietary fiber, 43 mg. calcium, 4 mg. iron, 12 mg. vitamin C, 0.4 mg. beta-carotene • **Serves 4**

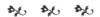

PASTA WITH ASPARAGUS AND TURKEY

- 8 ounces spaghetti or other long pasta
- 1 tablespoon olive oil
- 1 large garlic clove, minced
- 1½ pounds fresh asparagus spears, trimmed and cut diagonally into ½-inch pieces
- 1 large red bell pepper, diced
- 4 ounces smoked turkey (in one piece), diced
- ¼ teaspoon freshly ground black pepper
- 2 cups defatted reduced-sodium chicken broth
- 1 tablespoon cornstarch
- 1 ounce Parmesan cheese, grated

Asparagus stalks break naturally at the point where the stem becomes woody.

There are some parts of Italy where you needn't go to the market to buy asparagus—you can find thin spears of *asparagi di campo* (field asparagus) growing by the roadside. At the other extreme, luxuriously plump white asparagus is cultivated on farms in the Veneto region. This recipe is an amplification of *asparagi alla parmigiana:* The spears are tossed with spaghetti, smoked turkey, peppers and freshly grated Parmesan.

1 Bring a large covered pot of water to a boil over high heat.

2 Add the pasta to the boiling water, return to a boil and cook for 10 to 12 minutes, or according to package directions until al dente. Drain the pasta in a colander and transfer to a large bowl.

3 While the pasta is cooking, in a large skillet, warm the oil over medium heat. Add the garlic and cook, stirring occasionally, for 30 seconds. Add the asparagus, bell peppers, smoked turkey and black pepper; increase the heat to medium-high and cook, stirring occasionally, for 5 minutes.

4 Meanwhile, in a small bowl, whisk together the broth and cornstarch until the cornstarch dissolves.

5 Add the cornstarch mixture to the skillet, increase the heat to high and bring to a boil, whisking constantly. Continue to boil over high heat, whisking constantly, for 1 to 2 minutes, or until thickened.

6 Pour the sauce over the pasta, add the Parmesan and toss well to combine.

Preparation time 20 minutes • **Total time** 35 minutes • **Per serving** 356 calories, 7.6 g. fat (19% of calories), 2.3 g. saturated fat, 20 mg. cholesterol, 748 mg. sodium, 3 g. dietary fiber, 141 mg. calcium, 3 mg. iron, 88 mg. vitamin C, 1.5 mg. beta-carotene • **Serves 4**

HEAD START
Cut up the asparagus, bell peppers and turkey ahead of time, combine them and refrigerate in a covered bowl.

FOR A CHANGE
Other pastas that would work in this recipe are long fusilli, perciatelli (a thick, hollow spaghetti) and linguine.

BEEF AND MUSHROOM RIGATONI

¼ cup dried porcini mushrooms
   (½ ounce)

1 cup boiling water

6 ounces rigatoni pasta

12 ounces well-trimmed top round
   steak, thinly sliced

1 large garlic clove, minced

2 teaspoons olive oil

½ pound white mushrooms, sliced

1 bay leaf

½ teaspoon freshly ground black
   pepper

1 cup defatted beef broth

1 tablespoon cornstarch

2 tablespoons minced Italian
   parsley

Porcini are more commonly seen dried than fresh in this country. You can imitate the flavor of fresh porcini by cooking white button mushrooms with dried porcini.

1 Bring a large covered pot of water to a boil over high heat. Meanwhile, place the dried mushrooms in a large heatproof measuring cup. Pour the cup of boiling water over the mushrooms and let stand for 5 minutes, or until softened. Line a strainer with cheesecloth.

2 Using a slotted spoon, transfer the mushrooms to a small bowl. Place the strainer over the bowl and pour the soaking liquid through the cheesecloth, leaving the sediment in the bottom of the cup.

3 Add the pasta to the boiling water, return to a boil and cook for 12 to 14 minutes, or according to package directions until al dente. Drain the pasta in a colander and transfer to a large bowl.

4 While the pasta is cooking, spray a large, heavy no-stick skillet with no-stick spray and warm over medium-high heat. Add the steak and garlic to the skillet, and cook, stirring frequently, for 2 minutes, or until the steak is just cooked through. Transfer to a plate.

5 In the same skillet, warm the oil over medium heat. Add the white mushrooms, bay leaf and black pepper, and cook, stirring occasionally, for 4 to 5 minutes, or until the mushrooms release their juices.

6 Meanwhile, in a small bowl, whisk together the broth and cornstarch until the cornstarch dissolves. Add the softened dried mushrooms, the soaking liquid and the cornstarch mixture to the skillet, increase the heat to high and bring to a boil. Cook, stirring constantly, for 1 to 2 minutes, or until thickened.

7 Return the steak to the skillet, add the parsley and cook for 2 minutes, or just until heated through. Pour the sauce over the pasta and toss to combine.

Preparation time 15 minutes • **Total time** 35 minutes • **Per serving** 328 calories, 6.4 g. fat (18% of calories), 1.4 g. saturated fat, 48 mg. cholesterol, 462 mg. sodium, 1.9 g. dietary fiber, 23 mg. calcium, 5 mg. iron, 4 mg. vitamin C, 0.1 mg. beta-carotene • **Serves 4**

CHICKEN AND PASTA SALAD WITH GREENS

8 ounces penne rigati or
   gemelli pasta

1 tablespoon olive oil

10 ounces thin-sliced chicken
   cutlets

1 medium zucchini, cut in half
   lengthwise, then cut into
   thin slices

1 medium red bell pepper, diced

1 large garlic clove, minced

½ cup defatted chicken broth

3 tablespoons balsamic vinegar

2 teaspoons Dijon mustard

4 cups packed mixed greens
   (such as arugula and radicchio)

½ teaspoon cracked black pepper

¼ teaspoon salt

Chilled pasta salads are not found in traditional Italian cuisine, but this penne, chicken and vegetable mélange, dressed with a vinaigrette and served warm over mixed greens, takes its natural place among pasta *primi* (first courses). You'll probably want to serve something this hearty as a main dish, however.

1 Bring a large covered pot of water to a boil over high heat.

2 Add the pasta to the boiling water, return to a boil and cook for 10 to 12 minutes, or according to package directions until al dente. Drain the pasta in a colander, then transfer to a large bowl.

3 While the pasta is cooking, in large no-stick skillet, warm the oil over medium-high heat. Add the chicken cutlets and cook, turning once, for 4 to 5 minutes, or until the chicken is lightly browned and cooked through. Using tongs, transfer the chicken to a cutting board.

4 Add the zucchini, bell peppers and garlic to the skillet. Cook, stirring occasionally, for 5 minutes, or until the vegetables are just tender; remove to a plate with a slotted spoon.

5 To make the dressing, add the broth, vinegar and mustard to the skillet. Increase the heat to high and bring to a boil. Cook for 1 minute, or until slightly reduced. Remove the skillet from the heat.

6 Cut the chicken into thin strips and add to the large bowl with the pasta. Add the reserved vegetables, the greens, black pepper and salt. Pour the dressing over the salad and toss to combine.

Preparation time 15 minutes • **Total time** 35 minutes • **Per serving** 353 calories, 5.6 g. fat (14% of calories), 0.8 g. saturated fat, 41 mg. cholesterol, 392 mg. sodium, 3.3 g. dietary fiber, 108 mg. calcium, 4 mg. iron, 65 mg. vitamin C, 2.3 mg. beta-carotene • **Serves 4**

MARKET AND PANTRY
If you're not picking zucchini in your own garden, choose it carefully at the store. Look for medium-size, straight, firm, slender specimens with unblemished skins.

FOR A CHANGE
You can trade the zucchini for crookneck or pattypan summer squash (or substitute green beans or broccoli) and try turkey instead of chicken.

Orecchiette with Cauliflower

8 ounces orecchiette or small shell pasta

¼ cup unseasoned dry breadcrumbs

1 tablespoon olive oil

3 anchovy fillets, rinsed, patted dry and chopped

2 large garlic cloves, minced

¼ teaspoon crushed red pepper flakes

1 large head cauliflower, cut into small florets

1¼ cups defatted reduced-sodium chicken broth

⅔ cup frozen peas

1 ounce Parmesan cheese, grated

2 tablespoons chopped Italian parsley

*O*recchiette (little ears) are shaped like small, shallow cups, and here they nestle together nicely with the cauliflower (*cavolfiore*). The anchovies and Parmesan are two classic accents for this vegetable, which was brought to Europe from the Middle East in the 17th century.

1 Bring a large covered pot of water to a boil over high heat.

2 Add the pasta to the boiling water, return to a boil and cook for 10 to 12 minutes, or according to package directions until al dente. Drain the pasta in a colander.

3 Meanwhile, in a small saucepan, toast the breadcrumbs over medium heat for 2 to 3 minutes, or until golden brown; set aside.

4 In a large no-stick skillet, warm the oil over medium heat. Add the anchovies, garlic and red pepper flakes, and cook, stirring frequently, for 2 to 3 minutes, or until the garlic is golden brown.

5 Add the cauliflower, broth and peas to the skillet, increase the heat to high and bring to a boil. Reduce the heat to low, cover and simmer for 6 to 7 minutes, or until the cauliflower is tender.

6 Add the drained pasta, the Parmesan and parsley to the skillet, and toss to combine. Transfer the pasta mixture to 4 bowls or plates, and sprinkle with the toasted breadcrumbs.

Preparation time 20 minutes • **Total time** 35 minutes • **Per serving** 355 calories, 7.3 g. fat (18% of calories), 2.1 g. saturated fat, 7 mg. cholesterol, 547 mg. sodium, 4.8 g. dietary fiber, 167 mg. calcium, 4 mg. iron, 70 mg. vitamin C, 0.2 mg. beta-carotene • **Serves 4**

Oil-packed anchovies come in tins, like sardines, or in jars. Rinse the anchovies and pat them dry before using.

FOOD FACT

Anchovies are prized for their intense flavor. Salted anchovies were one of the predominant seasonings used in Roman times, and fermented anchovies form the base of the pungent Southeast Asian fish sauces *nuoc nam* and *nam pla*. Oil-packed anchovies have a distinctive—but not overpowering—flavor that adds a kick to familiar foods such as Caesar salad.

PASTA WITH SCALLOPS AND VEGETABLES

2 tablespoons olive oil

1 large garlic clove, minced

1 teaspoon salt

½ teaspoon cracked black pepper

3 large tomatoes, cut in half crosswise

4 large mushrooms, cut in half lengthwise

1 large red bell pepper, cut in half lengthwise, seeded and deribbed

1 medium yellow squash, cut in half lengthwise

1 medium zucchini, cut in half lengthwise

8 ounces medium pasta shells or spaghetti

12 ounces sea scallops, tough muscle removed

1 tablespoon minced fresh thyme or 1 teaspoon dried thyme

Fresh thyme sprigs, for garnish (optional)

A two-person team—one inside, one outside—could make quick work of this summer-perfect dish: While one cook mixes the basting sauce and boils the pasta, the other fires up the grill for the vegetables and scallops. A grilling basket makes it easy to cook the bite-size ingredients and keeps the food from falling into the fire.

1 Bring a large covered pot of water to a boil over high heat. Preheat the broiler or prepare the grill.

2 Meanwhile, in a small bowl, combine the oil, garlic, salt and black pepper; set aside.

3 Arrange the tomatoes, mushrooms, bell peppers, yellow squash and zucchini on the broiler-pan rack or in a grill basket. Brush the vegetables with the oil mixture. Broil or grill the vegetables 3 to 4 inches from the heat, without turning, for 8 to 10 minutes, or until tender. Transfer the vegetables to a cutting board to cool slightly. Leave the broiler on. When the vegetables have cooled, coarsely chop them and place in a large bowl.

4 While the vegetables are cooking, add the pasta to the boiling water, return to a boil and cook for 8 to 10 minutes, or according to package directions until al dente. Drain the pasta in a colander and transfer to the bowl with the vegetables.

5 Place the scallops on the broiler-pan rack or in the grill basket. Broil or grill the scallops 3 to 4 inches from the heat for 2 to 3 minutes, or until opaque and cooked through. Cut the scallops horizontally into thin slices and add to the bowl with the pasta and vegetables. Add the minced fresh thyme or dried thyme and toss to combine. Garnish each serving with thyme sprigs, if desired.

Preparation time 20 minutes • **Total time** 35 minutes • **Per serving** 400 calories, 9 g. fat (20% of calories), 1.2 g. saturated fat, 28 mg. cholesterol, 705 mg. sodium, 4.4 g. dietary fiber, 69 mg. calcium, 4 mg. iron, 78 mg. vitamin C, 1.5 mg. beta-carotene • **Serves 4**

ZITI WITH SAUSAGE, PEPPERS AND ONIONS

- 1 pound well-trimmed pork tenderloin, cut into chunks
- 2 large garlic cloves, quartered
- ½ teaspoon fennel seeds
- ¼ teaspoon crushed red pepper flakes, or more to taste
- ¼ teaspoon salt
- 2 teaspoons olive oil
- 1 medium red onion, cut in half lengthwise and thinly sliced
- 1 medium yellow onion, cut in half lengthwise and thinly sliced
- 1 medium red bell pepper, cut into very thin strips
- 1½ cups defatted chicken broth
- 6 ounces ziti pasta
- 1 teaspoon cornstarch

Those lucky enough to live near an Italian neighborhood can buy fresh sausage, a spicy (or sweet) blend of pork, garlic, fennel, red pepper and "secret" seasonings. But you can make a low-fat version of Italian sausage at home with a food processor—and, half an hour or so later, bring to the table a platter of sturdy ziti tossed with the sautéed sausage, sweet peppers and onions.

1 Bring a large covered pot of water to a boil over high heat.

2 Meanwhile, place the pork in a food processor and process until finely ground. Add the garlic, fennel seeds, red pepper flakes and salt, and pulse until blended.

3 Spray a large, heavy no-stick skillet with no-stick spray. Warm the skillet over medium-high heat. Add the pork mixture and cook, stirring to break up the clumps, for 5 to 7 minutes, or until the pork is cooked through and no longer pink. With a slotted spoon, remove the pork to a medium bowl.

4 In the same skillet, warm the oil over medium heat. Add the onions, bell peppers and ½ cup of the broth. Cover and cook, stirring occasionally, for 10 minutes. Uncover and cook, stirring occasionally, for 5 minutes longer, or until the onions and peppers are very tender.

5 While the onions and peppers are cooking, add the pasta to the boiling water, return to a boil and cook for 10 to 12 minutes, or according to package directions until al dente. Drain the pasta in a colander. Transfer the pasta to a large bowl.

6 In a small bowl, whisk together the remaining 1 cup of broth and the cornstarch until the cornstarch is dissolved. Return the pork to the skillet, increase the heat to high and stir in the cornstarch mixture. Bring to a boil, stirring constantly, and boil for about 1 minute, or until thickened. Add the pork mixture to the pasta and toss to combine.

Preparation time 20 minutes • **Total time** 45 minutes • **Per serving** 372 calories, 8 g. fat (19% of calories), 1.7 g. saturated fat, 74 mg. cholesterol, 577 mg. sodium, 2.7 g. dietary fiber, 43 mg. calcium, 3 mg. iron, 44 mg. vitamin C, 0.7 mg. beta-carotene • **Serves 4**

❧ ❧ ❧

TORTELLINI WITH CREAMY TOMATO SAUCE

2 teaspoons olive oil

2 garlic cloves, minced

1 large carrot, diced

1 medium onion, diced

1 medium celery stalk, diced

2 large tomatoes, seeded and coarsely chopped

½ teaspoon salt

¼ teaspoon freshly ground black pepper

12 ounces cheese tortellini

3 tablespoons part-skim ricotta cheese

3 tablespoons thinly sliced basil leaves

Whole basil leaves, for garnish (optional)

The plump little pasta pillows called tortellini were once only a special-occasion food: They're quite tricky to make, as you must first prepare the dough and stuffing, and then fill and fold the circles of pasta (being careful that the dough does not dry out and crack, and that you seal the tortellini so that they do not come apart when they're cooked). But now you can have them anytime, since fresh or frozen tortellini are sold in most supermarkets. They're delicious with this ricotta-enriched, basil-flavored sauce.

1 Bring a large covered pot of water to a boil over high heat.

2 Warm the oil in a large no-stick skillet over medium heat. Add the garlic, carrots, onions and celery, and cook, stirring occasionally, for 6 to 7 minutes, or until the vegetables begin to soften.

3 Add the tomatoes, salt and black pepper, increase the heat to high and bring to a boil. Reduce the heat to low, cover and simmer for 10 to 12 minutes, or until the vegetables are very tender.

4 Meanwhile, add the pasta to the boiling water, return to a boil and cook for 8 to 10 minutes, or according to package directions until al dente. Drain the pasta in a colander.

5 Pour the tomato sauce into a food processor and process until smooth. Add the ricotta cheese and continue to process until smooth and well blended. Return the sauce to the skillet and warm over low heat. Stir in the sliced basil.

6 Transfer the pasta to the skillet and toss with the tomato sauce until warmed through. Divide the pasta among 4 bowls and garnish with whole basil leaves, if desired.

If you halve the tomatoes crosswise (through the "equator"), it's easy to push out the seeds with your finger.

Preparation time 20 minutes • **Total time** 45 minutes • **Per serving** 345 calories, 9.5 g. fat (25% of calories), 3.4 g. saturated fat, 39 mg. cholesterol, 604 mg. sodium, 3.7 g. dietary fiber, 177 mg. calcium, 2 mg. iron, 21 mg. vitamin C, 4.6 mg. beta-carotene • **Serves 4**

❧ ❧ ❧

PASTA WITH SHRIMP, PEPPERS AND FENNEL

1 large red bell pepper, cut in half lengthwise, seeded and deribbed

1 large yellow pepper, cut in half lengthwise, seeded and deribbed

8 ounces spinach fettuccine

1 tablespoon olive oil

1 pound medium shrimp, peeled and deveined, with tails attached

1 large fennel bulb (about 1¼ pounds), cored and thinly sliced

1 large garlic clove, minced

1 cup defatted chicken broth

¼ cup fresh orange juice

1 teaspoon cornstarch

1 teaspoon grated orange zest

½ teaspoon salt

Roasted peppers add a tantalizing smoky flavor to this elegant entrée. Although you can buy roasted peppers in a jar, they're much tastier when you prepare them yourself (see Step 2).

1 Bring a large covered pot of water to a boil over high heat. Preheat the broiler. Spray the broiler-pan rack with no-stick spray.

2 Place the red and yellow bell peppers on the broiler-pan rack. Broil the peppers, cut-side down, 4 inches from the heat for about 5 minutes, or until the skins char. Transfer the peppers to a paper bag or a covered bowl to steam. Peel and dice the peppers; set aside.

3 Add the pasta to the boiling water, return to a boil and cook for 9 to 11 minutes, or according to package directions until al dente. Drain the pasta in a colander, then transfer the pasta to a warmed serving bowl.

4 While the pasta is cooking, in a large skillet, warm the oil over medium-high heat. Add the shrimp and cook, stirring frequently, for 2 minutes, or until the shrimp just turn pink. With a slotted spoon, transfer the shrimp to a plate.

5 Add the diced roasted peppers, the fennel and garlic to the skillet, and cook, stirring occasionally, for 2 minutes. Add the broth, increase the heat to high and bring to a boil. Reduce the heat to low, cover and simmer for 5 minutes, or until the fennel is tender.

6 Meanwhile, in a small bowl, whisk the orange juice and cornstarch until smooth.

7 Add the cornstarch mixture, orange zest, salt and shrimp to the skillet. Increase the heat to medium-high and bring to a boil. Cook, stirring, for 1 minute, or until the sauce thickens and the shrimp are cooked through.

8 Add the shrimp mixture to the pasta and toss to combine.

Preparation time 20 minutes • **Total time** 40 minutes • **Per serving** 395 calories, 8.2 g. fat (19% of calories), 1.3 g. saturated fat, 194 mg. cholesterol, 815 mg. sodium, 5.8 g. dietary fiber, 146 mg. calcium, 6 mg. iron, 90 mg. vitamin C, 1.2 mg. beta-carotene • **Serves 4**

❧ ❧ ❧

SKILLET CHICKEN, PASTA AND VEGETABLES

- **6 ounces penne rigati or ziti pasta**

- **8 ounces skinless, boneless chicken breast halves**

- **1 pound fresh spinach**

- **2 teaspoons olive oil**

- **2 garlic cloves, minced**

- **1 medium onion, finely chopped**

- **4 ounces fresh mushrooms, sliced**

- **1 can (14½ ounces) whole tomatoes with juice**

- **¼ teaspoon salt**

- **¼ teaspoon freshly ground black pepper**

- **2 tablespoons grated Parmesan cheese**

- **4 ounces part-skim mozzarella, shredded**

There's a shortcut to this dinner, which (with its topping of melted mozzarella) tastes like it baked for an hour in the oven: The whole thing is made in a skillet on the stovetop, and the cheese melts under the skillet's lid in less than 10 minutes.

1 Bring a large covered pot of water to a boil over high heat. Add the pasta to the boiling water, return to a boil and cook for 10 to 12 minutes, or according to package directions until al dente. Drain in a colander, rinse briefly under cold running water and drain again. Return the pasta to the cooking pot.

2 While the pasta is cooking, cut the chicken into ½-inch dice; set aside. Remove the tough stems from the spinach leaves and wash the leaves thoroughly. Pat the leaves dry and coarsely chop.

3 Spray a large no-stick skillet with no-stick spray. Add the oil and warm over medium-high heat. Add the chicken and cook, stirring frequently, for 4 to 5 minutes, or until the chicken is cooked through and no longer pink. With a slotted spoon, transfer the chicken to a medium bowl.

4 Add the garlic, onions and mushrooms to the skillet, and cook, stirring occasionally, for 5 minutes, or until the mushrooms release their juices.

5 Add the chopped spinach, the tomatoes and their juice, the salt and black pepper, stirring to break up the tomatoes with a spoon. Increase the heat to high and bring to a boil. Reduce the heat to low, cover and simmer for 5 minutes. Add the chicken and pasta to the skillet. Add the Parmesan and stir to combine.

6 Sprinkle the chicken, pasta and vegetables with the mozzarella. Cover the skillet and cook for 5 to 10 minutes, or until the mixture is hot and the cheese is melted.

Preparation time 20 minutes • **Total time** 50 minutes • **Per serving** 390 calories, 9.8 g. fat (23% of calories), 4 g. saturated fat, 51 mg. cholesterol, 588 mg. sodium, 5 g. dietary fiber, 353 mg. calcium, 5 mg. iron, 43 mg. vitamin C, 2.8 mg. beta-carotene • **Serves 4**

Poultry, Fish & Meat

❧ ❧ ❧

TASTE-TEMPTING ITALIAN DISHES

USING CHICKEN AND TURKEY,

SOLE AND SALMON,

LAMB AND PORK

CHICKEN BREASTS ARRABBIATA

1 tablespoon extra-virgin olive oil

1 cup chopped red bell peppers

1 cup chopped onions

¼ cup seeded, rinsed and chopped peperoncini

3 garlic cloves, crushed

½ teaspoon dried basil, crumbled

½ teaspoon sugar

½ teaspoon freshly ground black pepper

¼ teaspoon salt

⅛ teaspoon crushed red pepper flakes

3 cups coarsely chopped plum tomatoes

¼ cup defatted chicken broth

1 tablespoon no-salt-added tomato paste

1 pound skinless, boneless chicken breast halves (4 halves)

¼ cup chopped Italian parsley

*A*rrabbiata means "angry," and perhaps this dish got its name because it is somewhat "hot-tempered"—that is to say, spicy with peppers. There are four types of pepper in this recipe: sweet red bell peppers, pickled peperoncini, red pepper flakes and ground black pepper. Jars of peperoncini, slightly hot Italian pickled peppers, can be found in most supermarkets. Sometimes they're labeled "Tuscan peppers."

1 Preheat the broiler and broiler-pan rack.

2 In a large skillet, warm the oil over medium-high heat. Add the bell peppers, onions, peperoncini, garlic, basil, sugar, ¼ teaspoon of the black pepper, ⅛ teaspoon of the salt and the red pepper flakes, and stir to combine. Reduce the heat to medium and sauté for 3 to 4 minutes, or until the vegetables are tender.

3 Add the tomatoes, broth and tomato paste, increase the heat to medium-high and sauté for 2 to 3 minutes longer, or until the tomatoes start to release their juices.

4 Reduce the heat to medium, cover and simmer, stirring occasionally and mashing the tomatoes with a spoon, for 10 minutes, or until the tomatoes are reduced to a sauce.

5 Meanwhile, season the chicken on both sides with the remaining ¼ teaspoon black pepper and ⅛ teaspoon salt. Broil the chicken 4 to 5 inches from the heat for 5 minutes per side, or until browned and cooked through. Add the chicken to the tomato sauce, spoon the sauce over the chicken and bring to a simmer. Sprinkle with the parsley and remove from the heat.

6 To serve, place a piece of chicken on each of 4 plates and top with the sauce.

Preparation time 20 minutes • **Total time** 45 minutes • **Per serving** 220 calories, 5.6 g. fat (23% of calories), 0.9 g. saturated fat, 66 mg. cholesterol, 528 mg. sodium, 3.2 g. dietary fiber, 46 mg. calcium, 2 mg. iron, 83 mg. vitamin C, 1.6 mg. beta-carotene • **Serves 4**

❧ ❧ ❧

Preceding pages: Minted Lamb Chops with White Beans (recipe on page 73).

STEAK OREGANATA WITH MUSHROOMS

2 teaspoons grated lemon zest

2 tablespoons fresh lemon juice

2 tablespoons defatted chicken broth

1 tablespoon coarsely chopped fresh oregano leaves or ½ teaspoon dried oregano

2 garlic cloves, crushed

1 teaspoon extra-virgin olive oil

¾ teaspoon cracked black pepper

¼ teaspoon salt

1 pound well-trimmed boneless sirloin steak

16 large cremini or white mushrooms, stems trimmed even with the caps

Oregano or parsley sprigs, for garnish (optional)

Cremini do not look quite so "tame" and tidy as white button mushrooms.

You don't need a 12-ounce steak for a satisfying meal if you serve meaty mushrooms alongside. Sharing the plate with the sirloin slices here are *cremini* (flavorful pale-brown Italian button mushrooms). Use white mushrooms if you can't get cremini.

1 Preheat the broiler and the broiler-pan rack.

2 In a medium bowl, combine the lemon zest, lemon juice, broth, oregano, garlic, oil, black pepper and salt.

3 Rub 1 tablespoon of the herb mixture into one side of the steak. Turn the steak and rub with another tablespoon of the herb mixture.

4 Add the mushrooms to the remaining herb mixture and toss to coat.

5 Place the steak in the center of the broiler-pan rack. Place the mushrooms, stem-side down, around the steak. Pour the herb mixture remaining in the bowl over the steak and mushrooms.

6 Broil the steak and mushrooms 4 to 6 inches from the heat for 5 minutes. Turn the steak and mushrooms, and broil for 5 to 7 minutes longer, or until the steak is medium-rare and the mushrooms are lightly browned and tender. Transfer the steak to a cutting board and the mushrooms to 4 warmed plates. Let the steak rest for 5 minutes.

7 Carve the steak into thin slices and arrange on the plates with the mushrooms. Garnish with oregano or parsley sprigs, if desired.

Preparation time 10 minutes • **Total time** 35 minutes • **Per serving** 214 calories, 7.9 g. fat (33% of calories), 2.6 g. saturated fat, 76 mg. cholesterol, 228 mg. sodium, 1.7 g. dietary fiber, 26 mg. calcium, 5 mg. iron, 10 mg. vitamin C, 0 mg. beta-carotene
Serves 4

FOOD FACT
In Italy, when people go hunting, it's not always game they're after—sometimes the "prey" is wild mushrooms. Cremini are among the more common wild mushrooms, and today they are cultivated by American growers—which of course makes them more plentiful and cheaper.

COD STEAKS SICILIAN-STYLE

1 tablespoon plus 1 teaspoon
extra-virgin olive oil

1 medium onion, halved and
thinly sliced

1 cup thinly sliced fennel

2 garlic cloves, minced

½ teaspoon dried thyme, crumbled

¼ teaspoon salt

¼ teaspoon freshly ground
black pepper

1 tablespoon honey

1¼ teaspoons grated orange zest

1 tablespoon balsamic vinegar

1 can (16 ounces) crushed
tomatoes

½ cup fresh orange juice

3 tablespoons golden raisins

1¼ pounds cod steaks (4 steaks)

Chopped fresh parsley, for
garnish (optional)

Sicilian food might be characterized as assertive: The flavors are bold, the seasonings wonderfully varied. Rather than a simple poached fish with lemon juice, you'll encounter seafood dishes like this deeply savory braise of sturdy cod cooked with onions, fennel, garlic, tomatoes and orange juice. Honey, orange zest and raisins are surprising—but typically Sicilian—additions. If cod steaks are not available, use thick cod fillets—or halibut or haddock steaks. If you use fillets, check for doneness earlier—the baking time will be shorter for the thinner cuts.

1 Preheat the oven to 425°.

2 In a large, heavy no-stick skillet, warm the oil over medium-high heat until hot but not smoking. Add the onions, fennel, garlic, thyme, salt and black pepper, and sauté, reducing the heat slightly if necessary to keep the vegetables from sticking, for 3 to 4 minutes, or until the vegetables are just tender and lightly browned.

3 Stir in the honey and orange zest, and cook, stirring, for 30 seconds. Add the vinegar and simmer for 30 seconds, or until the vinegar is nearly evaporated and the vegetables are glazed.

4 Stir in the tomatoes, orange juice and raisins, and bring to a boil. Reduce the heat to medium-low and simmer for 5 minutes, or until the sauce is slightly thickened.

5 Place the cod steaks in a 9 x 9-inch nonreactive baking dish. Spoon the sauce over the fish. Bake, uncovered, for 12 to 15 minutes, or until the fish flakes easily when tested with a fork.

6 Transfer the fish and sauce to 4 plates. Sprinkle with chopped parsley, if desired.

Preparation time 15 minutes • **Total time** 45 minutes • **Per serving** 240 calories, 5.9 g. fat (22% of calories), 0.9 g. saturated fat, 54 mg. cholesterol, 418 mg. sodium, 2.3 g. dietary fiber, 87 mg. calcium, 2 mg. iron, 41 mg. vitamin C, 0.5 mg. beta-carotene • **Serves 4**

PORK TENDERLOIN WITH VEGETABLES

1 **pound small red potatoes, cut into 1-inch wedges**

3 **large carrots, cut into 1-inch chunks**

1 **tablespoon grated lemon zest**

2 **teaspoons dried rosemary, crumbled**

1 **teaspoon fennel seeds**

¾ **teaspoon cracked black pepper**

½ **teaspoon salt**

1 **pound well-trimmed pork tenderloin**

1 **tablespoon plus 1 teaspoon extra-virgin olive oil**

1 **large onion, cut into ½-inch-thick wedges**

4 **medium plum tomatoes, each cut into 4 wedges**

⅓ **cup defatted chicken broth**

Fresh rosemary sprigs, for garnish (optional)

Pork is very popular in Italy. Like all meats, it is typically eaten in modest portions, combined with generous amounts of vegetables, beans or pasta. Here, pork tenderloin, the leanest cut, is roasted along with potatoes, carrots, onions and tomatoes. Fennel seeds and rosemary add an unmistakably Italian fragrance and flavor.

1 Preheat the oven to 450°. Spray a heavy no-stick roasting pan or a broiler pan with no-stick spray.

2 Place the potatoes and carrots in a medium saucepan with cold water to cover. Cover the pan and bring to a boil over high heat. Reduce the heat to medium and simmer for 5 minutes, or until the potatoes are just tender. Drain the vegetables in a colander.

3 Meanwhile, in a large bowl, combine the lemon zest, rosemary, fennel seeds, black pepper and salt. Rub the pork tenderloin with 2 teaspoons of the herb mixture. Place the tenderloin in the center of the roasting pan or broiler pan and drizzle with 1 teaspoon of the oil; set aside.

4 Add the drained potatoes and carrots, the onion wedges and tomato wedges to the herb mixture remaining in the bowl. Add the remaining 1 tablespoon oil and toss to coat. Arrange the vegetables around the roast. Drizzle the vegetables with the broth.

5 Roast the pork and vegetables for 25 to 30 minutes, or until the pork is cooked through but still juicy in the center and the vegetables are tender and lightly browned on the edges. Transfer the pork to a cutting board.

6 Slice the pork on the diagonal, transfer to a platter and serve surrounded by the vegetables. Drizzle with the pan juices, and garnish with rosemary sprigs, if desired.

Preparation time 10 minutes • **Total time** 55 minutes • **Per serving** 342 calories, 9.9 g. fat (26% of calories), 2 g. saturated fat, 74 mg. cholesterol, 454 mg. sodium, 5.8 g. dietary fiber, 58 mg. calcium, 3 mg. iron, 39 mg. vitamin C, 12.8 mg. beta-carotene • **Serves 4**

SOLE FLORENTINE

1 tablespoon extra-virgin olive oil

1 cup diced red bell peppers

2 garlic cloves, minced

4 cups loosely packed chopped fresh spinach

½ teaspoon dried thyme, crumbled

¼ teaspoon salt

¼ teaspoon freshly ground black pepper

1 pound sole fillets (4 fillets)

¼ cup unseasoned dry breadcrumbs

1 large egg white

2 tablespoons grated Parmesan cheese

2 tablespoons dry white wine

1 tablespoon defatted chicken broth

Fresh thyme sprigs, for garnish (optional)

Florence is fabled for its food as well as for its art and architecture; and even humble spinach plays a role in the city's culinary glory. These spinach-stuffed sole fillets are baked in a small amount of wine, but you can substitute more broth if you wish.

1 Preheat the oven to 425°. Spray an 11 x 7-inch baking dish with no-stick spray.

2 In a large, heavy no-stick skillet, warm the oil over medium-high heat until hot but not smoking. Add the bell peppers and garlic, and sauté for 2 to 3 minutes, or until the peppers are tender. Transfer ¼ cup of the pepper mixture to a small bowl and set aside.

3 Increase the heat to medium-high heat and stir in the spinach, thyme, salt and black pepper. Cook, stirring, for about 1 minute, or until the spinach is wilted. Drain the spinach in a strainer, pressing down lightly to remove any excess moisture. Transfer the spinach to a medium bowl.

4 Cut the sole fillets in half lengthwise, removing any bones near the tops of the fillets.

5 Add the breadcrumbs, egg white and Parmesan to the spinach, and toss well. Spoon 2 rounded tablespoons of the spinach mixture onto the wide end of each piece of sole and roll up the fillet toward the narrow end. Place the rolls, seam-side down, in the prepared baking dish.

6 Sprinkle the rolls with the reserved bell pepper mixture, then drizzle with the wine and broth. Cover the baking dish with foil and bake for 10 to 12 minutes, or until the fish just flakes when tested with a fork and the filling is heated through.

7 Transfer 2 fish rolls with the bell pepper topping to each of 4 plates. Discard the pan juices. Garnish with fresh thyme sprigs, if desired.

Roll the fillets carefully, starting at the wide end and tucking in the filling as you go.

Preparation time 15 minutes • **Total time** 45 minutes • **Per serving** 207 calories, 6.6 g. fat (28% of calories), 1.4 g. saturated fat, 56 mg. cholesterol, 418 mg. sodium, 2.9 g. dietary fiber, 164 mg. calcium, 3 mg. iron, 72 mg. vitamin C, 4.3 mg. beta-carotene • **Serves 4**

MINTED LAMB CHOPS WITH WHITE BEANS

3 anchovy fillets, rinsed and patted dry

1 teaspoon extra-virgin olive oil

1½ teaspoons dried mint

½ teaspoon freshly ground black pepper

1¼ pounds well-trimmed loin lamb chops (4 chops)

2 cups coarsely chopped plum tomatoes

1 garlic clove, crushed

3 cups canned cannellini beans, rinsed and drained

2 tablespoons defatted reduced-sodium beef broth

¼ teaspoon salt

2 tablespoons chopped fresh mint

Mint sprigs and additional chopped fresh mint, for garnish (optional)

The mountainous region of Abruzzi is home to flocks of fat sheep. And fresh, tender lamb—*agnello*—is welcomed as one of the pleasures of spring. It may be roasted with garlic and mint, braised in wine or simply grilled. These thick chops are anointed with a paste of anchovies and mint before broiling; they're served with *cannellini*, plump white beans that are also grown in Abruzzi.

1 On a cutting board, finely chop the anchovies. Sprinkle with the oil, dried mint and ¼ teaspoon of the black pepper, then mash to a paste with the flat side of a chef's knife or a fork. Rub the anchovy paste evenly over both sides of the lamb chops. Place the chops on a plate, cover loosely with plastic wrap and set aside at room temperature for 15 minutes.

2 Meanwhile, preheat the broiler and broiler-pan rack.

3 While the chops stand, in a medium no-stick skillet, combine the tomatoes and garlic, and sauté over medium-high heat for 2 minutes, or until the tomatoes begin to give up their juices. Reduce the heat to medium, cover and cook for 2 to 3 minutes longer, or until the tomatoes are softened.

4 Stir in the beans, broth, salt, 1 tablespoon of the chopped fresh mint and remaining ¼ teaspoon black pepper, and bring to a simmer. Reduce the heat to medium-low, cover and simmer, stirring occasionally, for 10 minutes to blend the flavors.

5 While the beans are simmering, broil the lamb chops 5 to 6 inches from the heat for 4 to 6 minutes per side for medium.

6 To serve, spoon the bean mixture onto 4 warmed dinner plates and top each portion with a lamb chop. Sprinkle with the remaining 1 tablespoon chopped mint, and garnish with mint sprigs, if desired.

Preparation time 10 minutes • **Total time** 40 minutes • **Per serving** 369 calories, 11.2 g. fat (27% of calories), 3.3 g. saturated fat, 82 mg. cholesterol, 637 mg. sodium, 9.6 g. dietary fiber, 78 mg. calcium, 4 mg. iron, 20 mg. vitamin C, 0.4 mg. beta-carotene • **Serves 4**

TURKEY-SAGE CUTLETS WITH MUSHROOMS

⅓ cup dried mushrooms, preferably porcini (¼ ounce)

1 cup boiling water

1 pound thin-sliced turkey cutlets (4 cutlets)

¼ teaspoon salt

¼ teaspoon freshly ground black pepper

1½ teaspoons grated lemon zest

4 large fresh sage leaves plus ½ teaspoon coarsely chopped fresh sage

1 tablespoon all-purpose flour

1 tablespoon grated Parmesan cheese

1 tablespoon plus 1 teaspoon olive oil

12 ounces white button mushrooms, sliced

3 tablespoons dry Marsala

Marsala, a fortified wine produced in western Sicily, gives this dish a light winy "bouquet." If you prefer, substitute 4 teaspoons of grape juice plus 4 teaspoons of beef broth.

1 Place the dried mushrooms in a large heatproof measuring cup and pour the boiling water over them; let stand for 10 to 15 minutes, or until softened. Meanwhile, line a small strainer with cheesecloth.

2 With a slotted spoon, transfer the mushrooms from the soaking liquid to a cutting board and chop. Place the strainer over a small bowl and pour the soaking liquid through it, leaving the sediment in the cup. Reserve about ¼ cup of the soaking liquid.

3 Season the cutlets with the salt and black pepper. Rub one side of each cutlet with the lemon zest. Place a sage leaf on the bottom half of the zested side of each cutlet, then fold the cutlets in half crosswise. In a small bowl, combine the flour and Parmesan; dust the cutlets with the mixture.

4 In a large no-stick skillet, warm 2 teaspoons of the oil over medium-high heat. Sauté the cutlets, turning once halfway through cooking, for 6 to 8 minutes, or until browned and cooked through. Transfer the cutlets to a platter and cover loosely to keep warm.

5 Add the remaining 2 teaspoons oil to the skillet and warm over medium-high heat. Add the fresh mushrooms and softened dried mushrooms, and sauté for 2 minutes. Drizzle with 2 tablespoons of the reserved soaking liquid and the Marsala. Sauté for 2 to 3 minutes, or until the mushrooms are tender and the liquid is absorbed. Add a little more soaking liquid if the pan gets too dry. Pour any juices from the platter over the mushrooms, sprinkle with the chopped sage and simmer for 30 seconds.

6 Serve the cutlets topped with the mushrooms.

Preparation time 10 minutes • **Total time** 30 minutes • **Per serving** 220 calories, 6 g. fat (24% of calories), 1.1 g. saturated fat, 71 mg. cholesterol, 219 mg. sodium, 1.2 g. dietary fiber, 40 mg. calcium, 3 mg. iron, 4 mg. vitamin C, 0 mg. beta-carotene
Serves 4

❧ ❧ ❧

SHRIMP, POTATOES AND BROCCOLI RABE

12 ounces small red potatoes, quartered

1 large bunch broccoli rabe (about 1¼ pounds) or 4 cups broccoli florets

1 tablespoon plus 1 teaspoon extra-virgin olive oil

4 garlic cloves, minced

2 tablespoons chopped Italian parsley

¼ teaspoon crushed red pepper flakes

1 pound shrimp, peeled and deveined, with tails attached

2 tablespoons defatted chicken broth

½ teaspoon sugar

¼ teaspoon salt

Gather the broccoli rabe into a bunch so you can trim all the stems with one stroke of the knife.

The region known as Apulia forms the "heel" of the boot-shaped Italian peninsula. It juts out into the sea, with the Adriatic to the east and the Ionian Sea to the south and west. In Apulian cities such as Bari, fresh shellfish is sold at waterfront stands, to be eaten on the spot or taken home and cooked quickly and simply. This combination of shrimp, potatoes and robust greens captures the spirit of Apulian cuisine.

1 Place the potatoes in a medium saucepan with cold water to cover. Cover the pan and bring to a boil over high heat. Reduce the heat to medium and simmer for 8 to 10 minutes, or until the potatoes are fork-tender. Drain the potatoes in a colander, then return them to the saucepan. Cover to keep warm.

2 While the potatoes are cooking, trim the large, tough bottom stems from the broccoli rabe, if using. Cut the broccoli rabe into 2-inch pieces (you should have about 8 cups).

3 Fill a large, deep no-stick skillet with ½ inch of water. Cover and bring to a boil over high heat. Add the broccoli rabe or broccoli florets and return to a boil. Cook, uncovered, for 2 to 3 minutes, or until the broccoli is tender. Drain in a colander. Wipe the skillet dry.

4 In the same skillet, warm the oil over medium-high heat until hot but not smoking. Add the garlic, parsley and red pepper flakes, and sauté for 30 seconds, or until fragrant. Add the shrimp and sauté for 2 to 3 minutes, or until the shrimp are pink and opaque. With a slotted spoon, transfer the shrimp to a plate.

5 Add the drained potatoes and broccoli to the skillet. Add the broth, sugar and salt, and toss to mix well. Cook, tossing, for 1 to 2 minutes, or until heated through. Add the shrimp and toss to combine.

Preparation time 25 minutes • **Total time** 45 minutes • **Per serving** 254 calories, 6.8 g. fat (24% of calories), 1 g. saturated fat, 140 mg. cholesterol, 341 mg. sodium, 6 g. dietary fiber, 112 mg. calcium, 4 mg. iron, 109 mg. vitamin C, 1.3 mg. beta-carotene • **Serves 4**

❧ ❧ ❧

Parmesan Pork with Italian Slaw

1 tablespoon extra-virgin olive oil

1 pound well-trimmed boneless pork cutlets, pounded to ¼ inch thick (4 cutlets)

¼ teaspoon freshly ground black pepper

¼ teaspoon salt

1 large egg white

½ cup unseasoned dry breadcrumbs

1 tablespoon grated Parmesan cheese

1 tablespoon chopped fresh oregano

2 teaspoons defatted chicken broth

2 teaspoons red wine vinegar

¼ teaspoon sugar

1 medium head radicchio, coarsely shredded (4 ounces)

2 heads Belgian endive, cut crosswise on the diagonal into thin slices

1 large tomato, quartered and sliced crosswise

2 tablespoons chopped red onion

Fresh oregano leaves and oregano sprigs, for garnish (optional)

A surprising "slaw" of radicchio (an Italian chicory with thick, tight leaves that are a solid or variegated rosy red), Belgian endive, tomatoes and onions serves as a foil for these breaded, baked pork scallops. You can have the butcher pound the pork, or do it yourself with a wooden mallet or small, heavy skillet.

1 Preheat the oven to 450°. Coat a jelly-roll pan with 1 teaspoon of the oil.

2 Season the pork cutlets on both sides with the black pepper and ⅛ teaspoon of the salt.

3 In a glass pie plate or shallow bowl, lightly beat the egg white. On a plate, combine the breadcrumbs, Parmesan and 2 teaspoons of the chopped oregano.

4 One at a time, dip the cutlets into the egg white, letting the excess drip off, then dredge the cutlets in the breadcrumb mixture, pressing the mixture into both sides. Place the cutlets in a single layer in the prepared pan.

5 Drizzle the cutlets evenly with 1 teaspoon of the oil. Bake for 10 minutes, or until the undersides are lightly browned. Turn and bake for 5 minutes longer, or until browned and cooked through.

6 While the cutlets are cooking, make the dressing. In a medium bowl, whisk together the broth, vinegar, sugar, remaining 1 teaspoon each oil and oregano and the remaining ⅛ teaspoon salt.

7 Just before the cutlets are done, add the radicchio, endive, tomatoes and onions to the dressing, and toss to combine.

8 Transfer the cutlets to 4 plates and top with the salad. Garnish with oregano leaves and sprigs, if desired.

Preparation time 20 minutes • **Total time** 45 minutes • **Per serving** 262 calories, 10.9 g. fat (37% of calories), 3 g. saturated fat, 78 mg. cholesterol, 353 mg. sodium, 1.9 g. dietary fiber, 78 mg. calcium, 3 mg. iron, 16 mg. vitamin C, 0.5 mg. beta-carotene • **Serves 4**

PESTO SALMON

1¼ cups loosely packed fresh
   basil leaves

3 tablespoons defatted chicken
   broth

1 tablespoon blanched slivered
   almonds

1 tablespoon fresh lemon juice

2 teaspoons grated Parmesan
   cheese

2 teaspoons extra-virgin olive oil

¼ teaspoon salt

¼ teaspoon freshly ground
   black pepper

1 garlic clove, peeled

1 pound skinned salmon fillet, cut
   into 4 pieces

Lemon wedges and basil sprigs,
for garnish (optional)

Basil is one of the preeminent herbs in the Italian kitchen, and some of the finest basil is grown in Liguria, a coastal region of northern Italy. Pesto—a heady basil sauce—is the pride of Liguria and is used as a pasta sauce or as a last-minute addition to a bowl of minestrone. Here, a pesto made with almonds (rather than pine nuts) is slathered over salmon fillets before and after broiling.

1 To make the pesto, place the basil, broth, almonds, lemon juice, Parmesan, oil, salt and black pepper in a food processor. Turn the machine on, drop the garlic clove through the feed tube and process until puréed.

2 Place the pieces of salmon on a plate. Spoon 3 tablespoons of the pesto over the salmon and turn to coat both sides of each piece. Cover with plastic wrap and let stand at room temperature for 15 minutes. Reserve the remaining pesto at room temperature.

3 Meanwhile, preheat the broiler. Spray a jelly-roll pan with no-stick spray.

4 Place the salmon in the prepared pan. Spread any of the pesto remaining on the plate on top of each piece. Broil the salmon 4 to 5 inches from the heat for 6 to 8 minutes, or just until opaque in the center. (The cooking time will depend on the thickness of the fish.)

5 Transfer the salmon pieces to 4 dinner plates and top each piece with some of the reserved pesto. Garnish with lemon wedges and basil sprigs, if desired.

Preparation time 10 minutes • **Total time** 40 minutes • **Per serving** 222 calories, 11.6 g. fat (47% of calories), 1.7 g. saturated fat, 63 mg. cholesterol, 250 mg. sodium, 0.3 g. dietary fiber, 186 mg. calcium, 4 mg. iron, 7 mg. vitamin C, 0.4 mg. beta-carotene • **Serves 4**

FOR A CHANGE
The pesto would suit a number of other rich-fleshed fish, such as bluefish, snapper, tuna or swordfish. The fish could be broiled, grilled, steamed or poached.

ON THE MENU
Accompany the salmon with sautéed cherry tomatoes tossed with fresh herbs. If you pierce the tomatoes with a pin before heating them, they won't burst.

DRUMSTICKS WITH PEPPERS AND ONIONS

1½ pounds small chicken
   drumsticks, skinned
   (8 drumsticks)

1 large green bell pepper, cut into
   1-inch squares

1 large red bell pepper, cut into
   1-inch squares

1 medium red onion, cut into
   ½-inch wedges

8 pimiento-stuffed green olives,
   halved crosswise

4 garlic cloves, cut into thin slivers

3 tablespoons balsamic vinegar

½ teaspoon dried thyme, crumbled

¼ teaspoon freshly ground black
   pepper

¼ teaspoon salt

⅛ teaspoon crushed red pepper
   flakes

¾ cup water

¾ cup defatted chicken broth

¾ cup converted white rice

B raised chicken and vegetables is a simple enough recipe, but bright bell peppers, red onions and pimiento-stuffed green olives elevate this dish to company status. The flavors are as vivid as the colors, highlighted by lots of garlic and a splash of vinegar.

1 Preheat the oven to 425°.

2 Place the chicken, green and red bell peppers, onions, olives and garlic in a 13 x 9-inch baking dish. Drizzle with the vinegar, then sprinkle with the thyme, black pepper, salt and red pepper flakes. Toss to mix.

3 Bake the chicken and vegetables, uncovered, for 30 to 35 minutes, or until the chicken is cooked through and the vegetables are tender.

4 Meanwhile, in a medium saucepan, combine the water, broth and rice. Bring to a boil over high heat. Reduce the heat to low, cover and simmer for 20 minutes, or until the rice is tender and the liquid is absorbed.

5 Transfer the rice to a platter and top with the chicken, vegetables and pan juices.

Preparation time 15 minutes • **Total time** 50 minutes • **Per serving** 309 calories, 5.4 g. fat (16% of calories), 1 g. saturated fat, 83 mg. cholesterol, 613 mg. sodium, 2.4 g. dietary fiber, 64 mg. calcium, 3 mg. iron, 79 mg. vitamin C, 1 mg. beta-carotene
Serves 4

To slice the garlic without cutting yourself, stab the clove with a toothpick or skewer.

Hold the garlic in place on a cutting board as you slice it with a sharp paring knife.

VEGETABLES PARMESAN WITH MEAT SAUCE

1 medium eggplant

2 medium zucchini

2 teaspoons extra-virgin olive oil

½ teaspoon dried basil, crumbled

½ teaspoon dried oregano, crumbled

½ teaspoon freshly ground black pepper

¼ teaspoon salt

6 ounces lean beef top round, cut into chunks

3 garlic cloves, peeled

2 cans (8 ounces each) no-salt-added tomato sauce

1 large tomato, cut into ¼-inch-thick slices

1 ounce part-skim mozzarella cheese, shredded

1 ounce Parmesan cheese, coarsely grated

3 tablespoons unseasoned dry breadcrumbs

Classic eggplant parmigiana is loaded with fat—mainly because the eggplant is fried. Here, the vegetables bake, and even with a meat sauce and a cheese topping the dish is low in fat.

1 Preheat the oven to 475°. Spray 2 jelly-roll pans with no-stick spray.

2 Trim the eggplant and zucchini, and cut both into ¼-inch-thick slices. Place each vegetable in a separate medium bowl. In a small bowl, combine 1 teaspoon of the oil, ¼ teaspoon each of the basil, oregano and black pepper, and ⅛ teaspoon of the salt. Drizzle half the oil mixture over each vegetable and toss to coat well.

3 Place the eggplant in one of the prepared pans in a single layer and the zucchini in the other pan in a single layer. Place both pans in the oven and bake until the vegetables are tender and lightly browned (the zucchini should take about 10 minutes; the eggplant about 15 minutes). Remove from the oven; leave the oven on.

4 While the vegetables are cooking, in a food processor, combine the the beef, garlic, remaining ¼ teaspoon each basil, oregano and pepper, and the remaining ⅛ teaspoon salt, and pulse until finely ground.

5 In a medium, heavy no-stick skillet, warm the remaining 1 teaspoon oil over medium heat. Add the beef and cook, stirring, for 2 to 3 minutes, or until the beef loses its pink color. Stir in the tomato sauce and bring to a boil. Remove the skillet from the heat.

6 Spread ¾ cup of the meat sauce in the bottom of an 11 x 7-inch baking dish. Top with the eggplant and then the zucchini; cover with the tomato slices. Spoon the remaining meat sauce over the vegetables.

7 Sprinkle evenly with the mozzarella and Parmesan, then top with the breadcrumbs. Bake, uncovered, for 10 to 12 minutes, or until the cheeses are melted and the breadcrumbs are browned.

Preparation time 10 minutes • **Total time** 45 minutes • **Per serving** 246 calories, 8.6 g. fat (31% of calories), 3 g. saturated fat, 34 mg. cholesterol, 402 mg. sodium, 4.8 g. dietary fiber, 230 mg. calcium, 4 mg. iron, 36 mg. vitamin C, 1.3 mg. beta-carotene • **Serves 4**

Side Dishes

❧ ❧ ❧

THE GREENS, GRAINS AND

OTHER ACCOMPANIMENTS

THAT MAKE AN ITALIAN MEAL

COMPLETE

RICE WITH CONFETTI VEGETABLES

1½ cups water

¾ cup converted white rice

¼ teaspoon salt

⅛ teaspoon freshly ground black pepper

⅓ cup defatted chicken broth

1 cup shredded zucchini

1 cup shredded carrots

½ cup finely diced red bell pepper

¼ cup frozen green peas

¼ cup thinly sliced scallions

2 tablespoons chopped Italian parsley

½ teaspoon grated lemon zest

Citizens of Venice herald the arrival of spring with a bowl of *risi e bisi*—a slightly soupy mélange of rice and the tiniest of garden-fresh peas, flavored with ham, onions, parsley and Parmesan. Here, fluffy cooked rice is combined with peas (if your market stocks them, use the small frozen peas sold as petits pois) as well as shredded carrots, zucchini and bits of bell pepper and scallion. You can shred the carrots and zucchini by hand or with the shredding blade of a food processor.

1 In a medium saucepan, combine the water, rice, salt and black pepper, and bring to a boil over high heat. Reduce the heat to low, cover and simmer for 20 minutes, or until the rice is tender and the liquid is absorbed. Remove from the heat and set aside, covered.

2 In a large no-stick skillet, bring the broth to a boil over high heat. Add the zucchini, carrots, bell peppers, peas and scallions, and return to a boil. Reduce the heat to medium-low and simmer the vegetables, stirring frequently, for 3 to 4 minutes, or until tender.

3 Using a slotted spoon, transfer the vegetables to the pan with the rice. Add the parsley and lemon zest, and stir to combine.

Preparation time 15 minutes • **Total time** 40 minutes • **Per serving** 161 calories, 0.5 g. fat (3% of calories), 0.1 g. saturated fat, 0 mg. cholesterol, 242 mg. sodium, 2.4 g. dietary fiber, 45 mg. calcium, 2 mg. iron, 34 mg. vitamin C, 5.2 mg. beta-carotene • **Serves 4**

ON THE MENU
This side dish really brightens up a plate, so serve it with simple foods such as baked chicken or grilled fish. Because it's a combination of grain and vegetables, no other accompaniment is needed.

FOR A CHANGE
To transform the confetti rice into a main dish, add diced smoked turkey, ham or roast chicken breast; chunks of canned tuna or salmon; or rinsed and drained canned black beans or kidney beans.

Preceding pages: Parmesan-Baked Plum Tomatoes (recipe on page 93); Roasted Asparagus with Green Sauce (recipe on page 102); and Potato Cake with Sage and Garlic (recipe on page 94).

Spicy Green Beans with Anchovies

1 cup water

½ cup sun-dried tomatoes (not oil-packed)

1 garlic clove, peeled

1 pound green beans, trimmed and halved crosswise

2 tablespoons chopped Italian parsley

4 anchovy fillets, rinsed, patted dry and chopped

1 tablespoon balsamic vinegar

1 teaspoon extra-virgin olive oil

⅛ teaspoon salt

⅛ teaspoon freshly ground black pepper

⅛ teaspoon crushed red pepper flakes, or more to taste

This unusual vegetable combination could fit into several different places in a traditional Italian menu: Offer it as an appetizer, as a side dish, or, atop a bed of greens, as a salad course, served after the main dish. And the beans are equally good hot or cold. If anchovies are not to your liking, simply leave them out.

1 In a small saucepan, bring the water to a boil over high heat. Remove the pan from the heat, stir in the sun-dried tomatoes, cover and let stand for 8 to 10 minutes, or until the tomatoes are softened. Reserving 2 tablespoons of the soaking liquid, drain the tomatoes, and cut into small pieces with kitchen shears, or chop with a knife.

2 Pour ½ inch of water into a large, deep skillet; cover and bring to a boil over high heat. Add the garlic and cook for 1 minute; remove with a slotted spoon and set aside. Add the green beans to the skillet, return to a boil and cook, uncovered, for 5 to 6 minutes, or until the beans are tender. Drain the beans in a colander.

3 While the beans are cooking, in a serving bowl, combine the parsley, anchovies, vinegar, oil, salt, black pepper, red pepper flakes and the reserved 2 tablespoons soaking liquid. Using a garlic press, crush the garlic clove into the bowl and stir well to combine.

4 Add the beans and sun-dried tomatoes to the bowl, and toss to coat.

Preparation time 10 minutes • **Total time** 20 minutes • **Per serving** 73 calories, 1.6 g. fat (20% of calories), 0.3 g. saturated fat, 2 mg. cholesterol, 230 mg. sodium, 3.3 g. dietary fiber, 51 mg. calcium, 1 mg. iron, 18 mg. vitamin C, 0.5 mg. beta-carotene • **Serves 4**

FOOD FACT
Although you can now buy balsamic vinegar in supermarkets, its price will never be comparable with that of more common vinegars. (The finest balsamic vinegars inhabit the same price range as superb vintage wines.) Why spend dollars on a bottle of balsamic when you can get a pint of cider vinegar for pennies? Because no other vinegar has its sweet, complex flavor, and none is so carefully made. Only sweet trebbiano grapes go into balsamic vinegar, which is aged for at least 12 years in wooden casks. To get an authentic balsamic, bottled in Italy, look for a code on the label: Vinegars labeled API MO are from Modena, while those marked API RE are from Reggio.

PARMESAN-BAKED PLUM TOMATOES

8 medium plum tomatoes (about 1¼ pounds)

¼ teaspoon salt

⅛ teaspoon freshly ground black pepper

¾ teaspoon olive oil

16 small fresh basil leaves

2 tablespoons unseasoned dry breadcrumbs

1 tablespoon grated Parmesan cheese

As with so many other everyday kitchen tasks, your finger is the best tool for spreading the oil over the tomatoes.

Baked tomato halves are eaten all over Italy; plum tomatoes, which are less watery than spherical tomatoes, are especially good when cooked by this method. Some traditional recipes call for the tomatoes to bake in a deep pool of olive oil, but here the tops are rubbed with just a little oil. The baking time will depend to some extent on the ripeness of the tomatoes: If they are very ripe, check them for doneness a little sooner in the second phase of baking.

1 Preheat the the oven to 425°. Spray a jelly-roll pan with no-stick spray.

2 Cut the tomatoes in half lengthwise, trimming the stem ends, if desired. Arrange the tomatoes, cut-side-up, in a single layer in the prepared pan. Sprinkle the tomatoes with the salt and black pepper, then drizzle with the oil. With your finger, spread the oil and seasonings evenly over the surface of the tomatoes. Place a basil leaf on top of each tomato half.

3 In a cup, mix the breadcrumbs and Parmesan. Sprinkle the breadcrumb mixture evenly over the tomatoes. Bake for 10 minutes, or until the breadcrumbs are browned. Lay a sheet of foil over the tomatoes and bake for 10 minutes longer, or until the tomatoes are softened and heated through.

Preparation time 5 minutes • **Total time** 30 minutes • **Per serving** 57 calories, 2 g. fat (33% of calories), 0.4 g. saturated fat, 1 mg. cholesterol, 199 mg. sodium, 1.8 g. dietary fiber, 40 mg. calcium, 1 mg. iron, 25 mg. vitamin C, 0.5 mg. beta-carotene • **Serves 4**

❧   ❧   ❧

FOODWAYS

It's hard to imagine Italian food without tomatoes. However, as strongly as tomatoes are identified with Italian cuisine, they are New World natives and were not introduced to Italy until the 16th century. These first tomatoes were small and yellow, hence the Italian word for tomatoes— *pomodori,* or golden apples. By the 18th century larger red tomatoes had been bred and were beginning to be popular as a salad ingredient; only later did people begin to cook them. Today, tomatoes are grown all over Italy, but the best plum tomatoes—most of which go into cans—come from San Marzano.

POTATO CAKE WITH SAGE AND GARLIC

1 **pound thin-skinned potatoes, preferably yellow-fleshed**

2 **teaspoons olive oil**

¼ **teaspoon salt**

¼ **teaspoon cracked black pepper**

4 **garlic cloves, cut into thin slivers**

1½ **teaspoons slivered fresh sage or**
½ **teaspoon dried sage**

All over Europe you'll find irresistible variations on potatoes layered in a pan: This simple Italian dish is much like a French potato *galette* and a close cousin of Swiss *rösti*. However, when you taste the garlic and sage you'll immediately recognize it as an Italian creation. Yellow-fleshed potatoes, such as the Yukon Gold variety, make an especially pretty potato cake.

1 Preheat the oven to 450°. Generously coat an ovenproof 8- or 9-inch skillet or a 9-inch pie plate with no-stick spray.

2 By hand, or using the slicing blade of a food processor, cut the potatoes into very thin slices. Arrange the potato slices in overlapping concentric circles in the prepared pan.

3 Drizzle the oil evenly over the potatoes, sprinkle with the salt and black pepper then scatter the garlic on top. Sprinkle with the sage.

4 Bake for 30 minutes, or until the potatoes are crisp at the edges and tender in the center. Serve directly from the skillet or pie plate.

Arrange the potato slices in concentric rings in the skillet.

Preparation time 5 minutes • **Total time** 45 minutes • **Per serving** 124 calories, 3.5 g. fat (25% of calories), 0.3 g. saturated fat, 0 mg. cholesterol, 144 mg. sodium, 2 g. dietary fiber, 8 mg. calcium, 1 mg. iron, 18 mg. vitamin C, 0 mg. beta-carotene
Serves 4

KITCHEN TIP

If you buy small, uniformly sized potatoes, you can slice them in a food processor: Fit the processor with the slicing blade and drop the potatoes, one at a time, through the feed tube.

ON THE MENU

This crisp, sage-fragrant potato cake is worthy of a feast. Serve it with lemon-roasted chicken or game hens and herbed green and wax beans. For dessert, consider a lavish *tiramisù* (page 108).

BRAISED GREENS WITH BEANS

3 garlic cloves, crushed

1 teaspoon extra-virgin olive oil

3 cups torn escarole, rinsed

4 cups trimmed, loosely packed fresh spinach

1 bunch watercress, tough stems removed

1 can (19 ounces) red kidney beans, rinsed and drained

1 teaspoon balsamic vinegar

¼ teaspoon sugar

¼ teaspoon salt

⅛ teaspoon freshly ground black pepper

This hearty accompaniment for a light meal brings together three types of greens with meaty red kidney beans in garlicky olive oil; balsamic vinegar and a touch of sugar are added later to make a mild sweet-and-sour sauce. In Italy, many vegetables are cooked in olive oil with garlic. While sturdy vegetables like broccoli are usually blanched first, greens such as escarole, spinach and watercress, used here, can go right into the skillet, where they'll wilt in a matter of minutes.

1 In a large, heavy saucepan, combine the garlic and oil. Cook over medium-high heat, stirring constantly, for 1 to 2 minutes, or until the garlic is fragrant.

2 Add the escarole, increase the heat to high and cook, stirring frequently, for 1 to 2 minutes, or until wilted. Add the spinach and watercress, and cook, stirring frequently, for 1 to 2 minutes, or until all the greens are wilted and tender.

3 Add the beans, vinegar, sugar, salt and black pepper. Reduce the heat to medium-low and stir to combine. Cover and cook for 5 minutes, or until the beans are heated through and the flavors are blended.

Preparation time 15 minutes • **Total time** 30 minutes • **Per serving** 139 calories, 2.3 g. fat (15% of calories), 0.3 g. saturated fat, 0 mg. cholesterol, 395 mg. sodium, 9.4 g. dietary fiber, 189 mg. calcium, 4 mg. iron, 46 mg. vitamin C, 5 mg. beta-carotene • **Serves 4**

❧ ❧ ❧

MARKET AND PANTRY
Watercress is sold in fat little bunches, which are sometimes set in a tub of water to keep them fresh. Choose a bunch with crisp, dark green leaves and stems. For cooking, you need only cut off the tough bottom part of the stems; for salads, you just pinch off individual sprigs or leaves.

ON THE MENU
For an untraditional Italian vegetarian meal, pair this hearty vegetable dish with Soft Polenta with Gorgonzola (page 98). The garlicky greens provide a nice contrast for the cheese-laced polenta. Accompany the two dishes with crisp breadsticks and end the meal with fruit, hot drinks and biscotti.

SOFT POLENTA WITH GORGONZOLA

3½ cups cold water

½ teaspoon salt

1 cup yellow cornmeal

¼ cup 1% low-fat milk

1 ounce Gorgonzola cheese without rind, crumbled

1 tablespoon plus 1 teaspoon Neufchâtel cream cheese

½ teaspoon chopped fresh thyme or 1 tablespoon chopped parsley

¼ teaspoon freshly ground black pepper

Polenta, a sort of mush or porridge made from meal, can be prepared with oats, spelt, barley, millet, chestnut flour or buckwheat, but today it is most commonly made from coarse-ground yellow cornmeal. Corn was a gift from the New World to Europe, and cornmeal polenta did not become popular in Italy until the 17th century. Creamy and bland, polenta needs a jolt of flavor that is often supplied by a sharp cheese, such as pungent Gorgonzola.

1 In a large, heavy no-stick saucepan, combine the water and salt, and bring to a boil over high heat. Whisking constantly, add the cornmeal in a slow, steady stream.

2 Reduce the heat to medium-low and cook the cornmeal mixture, stirring frequently and vigorously with a wooden spoon, for 15 minutes, or until the cornmeal is thickened, glossy and very smooth. Stir in the milk and remove the pan from the heat.

3 Stir in the Gorgonzola and Neufchâtel, the thyme or parsley and the black pepper. Stir until the cheeses are melted. Serve immediately.

Preparation time 10 minutes • **Total time** 35 minutes • **Per serving** 171 calories, 4.1 g. fat (21% of calories), 2.3 g. saturated fat, 10 mg. cholesterol, 399 mg. sodium, 1.9 g. dietary fiber, 65 mg. calcium, 2 mg. iron, 1 mg. vitamin C, 0.2 mg. beta-carotene • **Serves 4**

❧ ❧ ❧

Gorgonzola, which originated near Milan, has a powerful flavor. One ounce is sufficient to flavor a big pot of polenta.

American Neufchâtel is a reduced-fat cream cheese. It gives the polenta a rich texture without adding a lot of fat.

BAKED FENNEL WITH TOMATO SAUCE

1 large or 2 medium fennel bulbs (about 1½ pounds)

1 can (14½ ounces) no-salt-added stewed tomatoes

1 tablespoon no-salt-added tomato paste

2 garlic cloves, crushed

1 tablespoon chopped fresh thyme leaves or ¼ teaspoon dried thyme

¼ teaspoon fennel seeds

¼ teaspoon dried tarragon, crumbled

⅛ teaspoon salt

⅛ teaspoon freshly ground black pepper

⅛ teaspoon crushed red pepper flakes

1 tablespoon grated Parmesan cheese

Fennel (*finocchio* in Italian) was once considered an appropriate food to be eaten at the end of a meal, perhaps to refresh the palate after a succession of heavy dishes. Crisp and sweet, with an aniselike fragrance, it would certainly succeed in that purpose. Fennel's sweet spiciness, however, is today more often tempered with savory ingredients, making it a tempting side dish for simple grilled poultry or fish. Here, fennel is slow-baked in an herbed tomato sauce and topped with Parmesan.

1 Preheat the oven to 425°.

2 Cut off and discard the stalks from the fennel. Halve the fennel bulb and cut into ¾-inch-thick wedges.

3 Put the fennel in a large saucepan and add cold water to cover. Cover the pan and bring to a boil over high heat. Reduce the heat to medium and simmer for 8 to 10 minutes, or until the fennel is fork-tender. Drain in a colander and arrange the fennel in a single layer in a 9 x 9-inch nonreactive baking dish.

4 While the fennel is cooking, in a small saucepan, combine the stewed tomatoes, tomato paste, garlic, thyme, fennel seeds, tarragon, salt, black pepper and red pepper flakes. Bring to a boil over medium-high heat, then immediately remove the pan from the heat.

5 Pour the tomato sauce over the fennel, sprinkle with the Parmesan and bake for about 15 minutes, or until the cheese is melted and the sauce is bubbly.

Preparation time 5 minutes • **Total time** 45 minutes • **Per serving** 62 calories, 0.7 g. fat (10% of calories), 0.2 g. saturated fat, 1 mg. cholesterol, 250 mg. sodium, 3.9 g. dietary fiber, 127 mg. calcium, 2 mg. iron, 30 mg. vitamin C, 0.5 mg. beta-carotene • **Serves 4**

SUBSTITUTION

If fennel is not available, you can cook celery in the same fashion: The fennel seeds in the sauce will give the celery a mild fennel flavor.

NUTRITION NOTE

Fennel is a good source of calcium, roughly comparable to such better-known sources for that mineral as spinach, beet greens and collards.

Roasted Asparagus with Green Sauce

- 1 **pound fresh asparagus spears, trimmed**
- 1 **teaspoon grated lemon zest**
- 1 **teaspoon extra-virgin olive oil**
- ¼ **teaspoon salt**
- ¼ **teaspoon freshly ground black pepper**
- ⅓ **cup packed Italian parsley sprigs**
- ⅓ **cup sliced scallions**
- 2 **tablespoons defatted chicken broth**
- 2 **garlic cloves, sliced**
- ½ **teaspoon dried tarragon, crumbled**
- ⅔ **cup plain nonfat yogurt**
- 1 **tablespoon fresh lemon juice**
- 1 **tablespoon low-fat mayonnaise**
- **Lemon wedges (optional)**

Asparagus has been grown in Italy since Roman times; the asparagus grown in Ravenna, in the Emilia-Romagna region, was praised by the ancients, including famed historian Pliny the Elder. Here is a pleasing way to present the succulent spears (which may be served hot, warm or chilled): with a creamy lemon-herb sauce. Roasting, an unusual method for green vegetables, cooks the asparagus slowly and evenly. Note that the cooking time will depend on the thickness (or thinness) of the asparagus stalks.

1 Preheat the oven to 425°. Spray an 11 x 7-inch baking dish with no-stick spray.

2 Arrange the asparagus in the prepared pan. Sprinkle with the lemon zest, then drizzle with the oil. Sprinkle with ⅛ teaspoon each of the salt and black pepper. Turn the asparagus to coat it with the seasonings. Bake, turning the asparagus a few times, for 20 to 25 minutes, or until the spears are tender.

3 Meanwhile, in a small skillet, combine the parsley, scallions, broth, garlic and tarragon. Bring to a boil over high heat, then cover and simmer, stirring occasionally, for 3 to 4 minutes, or until the scallions are tender.

4 Transfer the mixture to a food processor. Add the yogurt, lemon juice, mayonnaise and the remaining ⅛ teaspoon each salt and black pepper, and purée until smooth. Transfer to a small bowl.

5 Serve the asparagus with the green sauce on the side. Offer lemon wedges, if desired.

Preparation time 15 minutes • **Total time** 30 minutes • **Per serving** 71 calories, 2 g. fat (26% of calories), 0.2 g. saturated fat, 1 mg. cholesterol, 238 mg. sodium, 1.6 g. dietary fiber, 122 mg. calcium, 1 mg. iron, 44 mg. vitamin C, 0.8 mg. beta-carotene • **Serves 4**

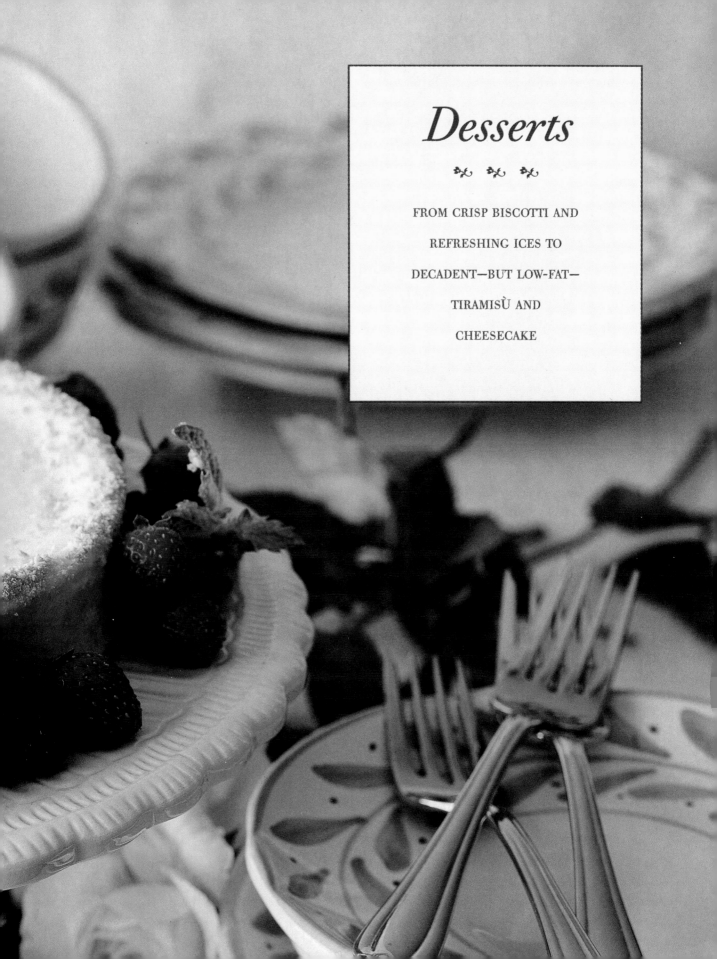

Desserts

❧ ❧ ❧

FROM CRISP BISCOTTI AND
REFRESHING ICES TO
DECADENT—BUT LOW-FAT—
TIRAMISÙ AND
CHEESECAKE

AMARETTI-STUFFED BAKED PEACHES

4 large ripe peaches (about 1¾ pounds)

½ cup coarsely crushed amaretti cookies (8 large amaretti cookies or 42 miniature amaretti cookies)

2 tablespoons raspberry all-fruit preserves

¼ teaspoon grated lemon zest

Lemon balm or mint leaves, for garnish (optional)

The mountains and hills of the Piedmont, in northern Italy, are home to lush orchards that produce apples, pears, cherries and peaches. *Pesche ripiene alla piemontese* is a classic peach dessert from this region. The amaretti—crisp macaroons—have an intriguing sweet-and-bitter almond flavor: Peaches and almonds belong to the same botanical family, which helps explain why their flavors complement each other so beautifully.

1 Preheat the oven to 400°.

2 Cut the peaches in half lengthwise (do not peel). Remove and discard the stones. Scoop out a small amount of pulp from the center of each peach half and coarsely chop the pulp.

3 Place the chopped peach pulp in a small bowl. Add the amaretti, raspberry preserves and lemon zest, and stir to combine.

4 Spoon some of the amaretti mixture into the center of each peach half. Place the peach halves in an 11 x 7-inch baking pan and bake for 20 to 25 minutes, or until the peaches are tender. Garnish with lemon balm or mint leaves, if desired.

Amaretti are available in large and small sizes. The larger cookies come packed in pairs and are wrapped in pretty, old-fashioned paper, which makes them an attractive dessert in themselves.

Preparation time 10 minutes • **Total time** 45 minutes • **Per serving** 119 calories, 1 g. fat (7% of calories), 0 g. saturated fat, 0 mg. cholesterol, 4 mg. sodium, 2.4 g. dietary fiber, 8 mg. calcium, 0 mg. iron, 10 mg. vitamin C, 0.5 mg. beta-carotene • **Serves 4**

FOOD NOTE
Herb leaves make pretty garnishes for desserts. Shown opposite are leaves of lemon balm, which exude a lemony fragrance when the leaves are crushed. Mint leaves are also often used for garnishing desserts. In addition to the familiar spearmint and peppermint, try apple, orange and pineapple mint, all faintly scented with their namesake fruits.

Preceding pages: Ricotta Cheesecake (recipe on page 116).

TIRAMISÙ

6 ounces Neufchâtel cream cheese, softened

6 ounces fat-free cream cheese, softened

⅔ cup reduced-fat sour cream

⅔ cup fat-free sour cream

½ cup sugar

2 packages (3 ounces each) ladyfingers

¾ cup hot water

1 tablespoon instant espresso coffee granules (or omit hot water and use ¾ cup strong decaf or regular coffee)

2 tablespoons rum or ¼ teaspoon imitation rum extract

½ teaspoon unsweetened cocoa powder

1 square (1 ounce) semisweet chocolate

To make chocolate curls, warm the bar of chocolate in your hands for a few minutes, then pare off shavings with a swivel-bladed vegetable peeler.

A newcomer to the Italian culinary scene, the fabulous cocoa-crowned *tiramisù* has enjoyed quite a vogue on restaurant menus. The layers consist of espresso-and-rum-soaked ladyfingers and *crema de mascarpone* (a fluffy, super-rich cream cheese mixed with egg yolks and sugar). The lower-fat and fat-free cheeses and sour creams used in this recipe cut lots of calories and fat—so you can have your tiramisù and eat your dinner, too.

1 In a large bowl, with an electric mixer at medium speed, beat the Neufchâtel and the fat-free cream cheeses together until smooth. Add the reduced-fat and fat-free sour creams and the sugar, and beat until smooth; set aside.

2 Split the ladyfingers in half lengthwise. In a small bowl, combine the hot water and espresso granules, if using, and the rum or rum extract. Quickly dip half the ladyfinger halves, cut-side down, into the espresso mixture. Place the ladyfingers, dipped-side down, in the bottom of a 9-inch-square baking dish or pan, overlapping them, if necessary, to fit. Spread half of the cream cheese mixture evenly over the ladyfingers.

3 Dip the remaining ladyfinger halves into the remaining espresso mixture, then place them, dipped-side down, on top of the cream cheese. Spread the remaining cream cheese mixture on top of the ladyfingers. Cover the pan with plastic wrap and refrigerate for 2 to 3 hours, or until chilled.

4 Just before serving, sprinkle the tiramisù with the cocoa powder and top with chocolate curls (see directions at left).

Preparation time 5 minutes • **Total time** 30 minutes plus chilling time • **Per serving** 236 calories, 8.6 g. fat (33% of calories), 4.9 g. saturated fat, 56 mg. cholesterol, 323 mg. sodium, 0.2 g. dietary fiber, 114 mg. calcium, 1 mg. iron, 0 mg. vitamin C, 0.4 mg. beta-carotene • **Serves 9**

ORANGE-ALMOND BISCOTTI

½ cup blanched slivered almonds

1¼ cups all-purpose flour

⅓ cup sugar

½ teaspoon baking soda

⅛ teaspoon salt

1 large egg

1 large egg white

1 teaspoon grated orange zest

Using a very sharp, serrated knife, cut the partially baked biscotti logs into slices with a gentle sawing motion.

The Italian equivalent of cookies and milk is biscotti with a glass of sweet wine (such as a Tuscan *vin santo*), served as a snack at any time of day. Because biscotti are baked twice, they are quite hard and are most enjoyable when dipped—into wine, coffee, tea, milk or cocoa. They're also good with a fresh fruit salad or sorbet.

1 Preheat the oven to 350°. Spray a baking sheet with no-stick spray.

2 Place the almonds in a single layer in a small baking pan and toast in the oven for 5 to 8 minutes, or until lightly browned. Remove from the oven and set aside; reduce the oven temperature to 325°.

3 In a food processor, combine the flour, sugar, baking soda and salt, and process until well mixed. Add the egg, egg white and orange zest, and process until the dough begins to leave the sides of the work bowl. Transfer the dough to a work surface.

4 Sprinkle the dough with the toasted almonds, then knead the almonds into the dough. Divide the dough in half and, with your hands, roll each half into a 10-inch-long log. Gently transfer the logs to the prepared baking sheet. Flatten each log slightly. Bake for 20 to 25 minutes, or until the bottoms are lightly browned.

5 Transfer the logs to a wire rack to cool for a few minutes. Slice each log diagonally into ½-inch-thick slices. Transfer the biscotti, cut-side down, to the baking sheet and bake, turning once, for 15 minutes, or until the biscotti are dry and lightly browned all over.

Preparation time 5 minutes • **Total time** 1 hour • **Per cookie** 44 calories, 1.4 g. fat (29% of calories), 0.2 g. saturated fat, 7 mg. cholesterol, 34 mg. sodium, 0.2 g. dietary fiber, 8 mg. calcium, 0.3 mg. iron, 0.1 mg. vitamin C, 0 mg. beta-carotene • **Makes 30 cookies**

KITCHEN TIP
You can also make these biscotti without a food processor: Combine the flour, sugar, baking soda and salt in a large bowl, and stir with a whisk until well mixed. In a small bowl, beat together the egg, egg white and orange zest until well-combined, then add this mixture to the dry ingredients. Using a wooden spoon and then your hands, mix to form a dough.

PLUM-BERRY CROSTATA

½ cup plus 2 tablespoons all-purpose flour

½ cup yellow cornmeal

¼ cup plus 2 tablespoons sugar

¼ teaspoon salt

¼ cup plus 2 tablespoons reduced-calorie tub margarine (6 grams of fat per tablespoon)

2 medium plums, pitted and sliced

1 pint strawberries, hulled and sliced

The pastry dough is somewhat fragile, but a thin metal spatula will enable you to fold the edge of the dough over the filling. If the dough cracks, simply press it back together.

A *crostata* can take many forms: Sometimes it's a lattice-topped tart, sometimes a sort of deep-dish pie, and sometimes a kind of shortcake. For this free-form *crostata,* you roll out the dough, top it with sliced plums and strawberries, and then gently fold the edges of the pastry around the fruits. For a shortcut, place the disk of chilled dough directly on the baking sheet, cover the dough with a sheet of wax paper and roll it out right on the baking sheet.

1 In a food processor, combine the flour, cornmeal, ¼ cup of the sugar and the salt, and process until well combined. Add the margarine and process until the dough begins to leave the sides of the work bowl. Remove the dough and press into a flattened disk. Wrap the dough with plastic wrap and refrigerate for 30 minutes, or until chilled.

2 Preheat the oven to 425°. Line a large baking sheet with foil or parchment paper and spray with no-stick spray.

3 Place the dough between 2 pieces of wax paper, and, using a rolling pin, roll into a 12-inch round. Carefully peel off the top piece of wax paper, invert the dough onto the prepared baking sheet and peel off the remaining wax paper. Arrange the plums and strawberries in a pretty pattern on top of the dough, leaving a 1½-inch border of dough all around. Using a metal spatula, carefully lift the dough border back over the fruits to form a rim. Sprinkle the fruits with the remaining 2 tablespoons of sugar.

4 Bake the crostata for 15 to 20 minutes, or until the pastry is golden brown and the fruits are tender. Transfer the baking sheet to a wire rack and allow the crostata to cool on the baking sheet for 10 minutes. Carefully transfer the crostata to a platter or cut into wedges directly on the baking sheet.

Preparation time 10 minutes • **Total time** 45 minutes plus chilling and standing time • **Per serving** 221 calories, 7.3 g. fat (30% of calories), 1 g. saturated fat, 0 mg. cholesterol, 221 mg. sodium, 2.8 g. dietary fiber, 12 mg. calcium, 1 mg. iron, 32 mg. vitamin C, 0.4 mg. beta-carotene • **Serves 6**

SWEET FRUIT-FILLED RAVIOLI

Dough

1¼ cups cake flour

¼ cup sugar

¼ teaspoon salt

¼ cup reduced-calorie tub margarine (6 grams of fat per tablespoon)

1 large egg

Filling

2 large dried figs

¼ cup raisins

1½ teaspoons sweet Marsala wine or orange juice

½ ounce unsweetened chocolate, finely chopped

¼ teaspoon grated lemon zest

¼ teaspoon grated orange zest

Confectioners' sugar, for topping (optional)

Hold the Parmesan—these are *ravioli dolci* (sweet ravioli) from Apulia, a fitting dessert for this southern region where pasta-eating amounts to an obsession. A mixture of dried fruits and chocolate fills these plump little pastries.

1 To make the dough, in a food processor, combine the flour, sugar and salt, and process until blended. Add the margarine and process until the mixture resembles coarse cornmeal. Add the egg and process until the dough pulls away from the sides of the work bowl. Remove the dough and shape it into a flattened disk. Wrap the dough in plastic wrap and refrigerate for 30 minutes. Wash the work bowl.

2 To make the filling, place the figs in a small saucepan with enough water to cover and bring to a boil over high heat. Reduce the heat to low and simmer for 8 to 10 minutes, or until the figs are softened. Drain the figs in a colander. Remove and discard the stems.

3 In the food processor, combine the figs and raisins, and process until finely chopped. Transfer the chopped fruits to a small bowl. Stir in the Marsala or orange juice, chocolate, lemon zest and orange zest.

4 Preheat the oven to 350°. Spray a large baking sheet with no-stick spray.

5 On a floured surface, using a floured rolling pin, roll half the dough into a ⅛-inch-thick round. Using a 2½-inch round cookie cutter, cut the dough into 12 circles. Spoon a rounded ½ teaspoon of the fruit filling onto half of each circle of dough. Fold the dough over the filling, pressing the edges together with the tines of a fork to seal. Repeat with the remaining dough and trimmings. Place the ravioli on the prepared baking sheet and bake for 10 to 12 minutes, or until golden. Transfer the ravioli to a wire rack to cool. If desired, just before serving, place some confectioners' sugar in a strainer and sprinkle lightly over the ravioli.

Preparation time 15 minutes • **Total time** 55 minutes plus chilling time • **Per cookie** 55 calories, 1.7 g. fat (27% of calories), 0.4 g. saturated fat, 9 mg. cholesterol, 47 mg. sodium, 0.4 g. dietary fiber, 7 mg. calcium, 1 mg. iron, 0 mg. vitamin C, 0.1 mg. beta-carotene • **Makes 24 cookies**

RICOTTA CHEESECAKE

Crust

- ½ cup graham cracker crumbs
- 1 tablespoon sugar

Filling

- ¾ cup fat-free ricotta cheese
- ¾ cup part-skim ricotta cheese
- 4 ounces fat-free cream cheese, softened
- 4 ounces Neufchâtel cream cheese, softened
- ⅔ cup sugar
- ¼ cup all-purpose flour
- 1 large egg
- 2 large egg whites
- 2 teaspoons vanilla extract
- 2 teaspoons fresh lemon juice
- 2 teaspoons fresh orange juice
- 1 teaspoon grated lemon zest
- 1 teaspoon grated orange zest
- ½ cup golden raisins

Edible flowers, for garnish (optional)

Distinctly different from dense New York-style cheesecake, this updated version of the Italian *crostata di ricotta* is made with low-fat and fat-free cheeses. The light yet creamy filling has a bright citrus flavor and is studded with golden raisins. In place of the traditional pastry crust, this cake has a crumb crust for a substantial savings in calories and fat. And while the process may appear time consuming, you really spend only about 15 minutes putting the cake together—the rest of the time goes to baking and chilling.

1 Preheat the oven to 325°. Spray the bottom and sides of an 8-inch springform pan with no-stick spray.

2 To make the crust, in a small bowl, combine the graham cracker crumbs and sugar. Transfer the crumb mixture to the prepared pan. Tilt and rotate the pan to coat the bottom and sides with the crumb mixture; set aside.

3 To make the filling, place a sieve or fine-mesh strainer over the large bowl of an electric mixer. Press the fat-free and part-skim ricotta cheeses through the sieve or strainer to remove graininess. With the electric mixer at medium speed, beat the ricotta cheeses until smooth. Add the fat-free and Neufchâtel cream cheeses, and beat until smooth. Add the sugar, flour, egg, egg whites, vanilla, lemon juice, orange juice, lemon zest and orange zest, and beat well. Stir in the raisins.

4 Pour the filling into the prepared pan. Bake for 45 to 50 minutes, or until the cheesecake is puffed at the edges but still slightly wobbly in the center. Turn off the oven and leave the cheesecake in the oven with the door closed for 30 minutes. Transfer the pan to a wire rack to cool completely. Cover and refrigerate for 3 to 4 hours, or until chilled.

5 When the cake is chilled, run a knife around the inside of the pan and remove the pan. Garnish the top of the cheesecake with edible flowers, if desired.

Preparation time 15 minutes • **Total time** 1 hour 10 minutes plus standing and chilling time • **Per serving** 263 calories, 6.6 g. fat (23% of calories), 3.4 g. saturated fat, 46 mg. cholesterol, 247 mg. sodium, 0.8 g. dietary fiber, 236 mg. calcium, 1 mg. iron, 2 mg. vitamin C, 0.4 mg. beta-carotene • **Serves 8**

Honeydew-Lime Granita

1 cup water

½ cup sugar

1 very ripe honeydew melon
(about 4 pounds)

1 tablespoon lime juice

2 teaspoons grated lime zest

2 cups raspberries, strawberries
and/or blackberries

Most commonly made in lemon or coffee flavors, granitas are refreshingly crunchy sorbets. You don't need an ice-cream machine to freeze them: Just put the sweetened fruit mixture in a metal pan and scrape the ice crystals with a fork as they form. Fresh berries are a perfect—and perfectly nutritious—topping.

1 Place a 13 x 9-inch metal baking pan in the freezer. In a medium saucepan, combine the water and sugar, and bring to a simmer over medium heat. Cook, stirring occasionally, for about 3 minutes, or until the sugar completely dissolves. Remove the pan from the heat and refrigerate to cool completely.

2 Meanwhile, cut the honeydew in half, discard the seeds and scoop out the pulp. Place the pulp in a food processor and process until smooth. Add the cooled sugar syrup, the lime juice and lime zest, and process just until combined.

3 Pour the melon mixture into the chilled baking pan. Freeze for about 30 minutes, or until ice crystals form around the edges. Using a fork, stir well to incorporate the ice. Continue freezing, stirring every 30 minutes or so, for about 2½ to 3 hours, or until the mixture is completely frozen.

4 To serve, spoon the ice into 4 dessert glasses or bowls and top each with some berries.

To achieve the desired crunchy texture, periodically stir the ice crystals from the edges of the pan into the center.

Preparation time 5 minutes • **Total time** 15 minutes plus chilling time • **Per serving** 101 calories, 0.3 g. fat (2% of calories), 0 g. saturated fat, 0 mg. cholesterol, 11 mg. sodium, 2.4 g. dietary fiber, 14 mg. calcium, 0 mg. iron, 34 mg. vitamin C, 0 mg. beta-carotene • **Serves 8**

MARKET AND PANTRY
To get a really delicious honeydew, look for a melon that's a yellowy cream color rather than a flat greenish white. The skin should be velvety, not slick and smooth. Tiny "freckles" on the skin are also a sign of sweetness. The blossom end should be sweetly fragrant.

FOR A CHANGE
Cantaloupe makes an equally delicious granita; adjust the sugar and lime to taste.

Hazelnut Meringue Cookies

¼ **cup hazelnuts**

½ **cup sugar**

¼ **cup all-purpose flour**

2 **large egg whites**

   Pinch of salt

½ **teaspoon vanilla extract**

Rubbing the toasted hazelnuts between your hands in a kitchen towel should remove most of the skin from the nuts.

Sicily is home to a staggering variety of sweets—eye-fooling marzipan fruits, pastries bursting with cream, the lavish layered ice-cream cake called *cassata*—many of them made with the local fruits and nuts. These feather-light *spumette di nocciole* are among the more modest Sicilian desserts; they're delicious alone or with fruits or fruit drinks.

1 Preheat the oven to 350°. Spray 2 large baking sheets with no-stick spray.

2 Place the hazelnuts in a jelly-roll pan. Bake the hazelnuts for 10 to 15 minutes, or until the skins begin to loosen and the nuts are toasted. Place the nuts in a kitchen towel and rub to remove the skins.

3 Transfer the nuts to a food processor, add the sugar and process until the nuts are finely ground. Transfer the nuts to a medium bowl, add the flour and stir to combine.

4 In a large bowl, with an electric mixer at high speed, beat the egg whites and salt until stiff peaks form. Fold in the hazelnut mixture and the vanilla.

5 Using 2 teaspoons of batter for each cookie, drop the batter onto the prepared baking sheets, leaving 1½ inches of space between cookies. Bake both sheets at once, switching the baking sheets on the racks halfway through baking, for 5 to 6 minutes, or until the edges of the cookies are browned. Remove the baking sheets from the oven and transfer the cookies to a rack to cool.

Preparation time 5 minutes • **Total time** 45 minutes • **Per cookie** 38 calories, 1.1 g. fat (27% of calories), 0.1 g. saturated fat, 0 mg. cholesterol, 12 mg. sodium, 0.1 g. dietary fiber, 3 mg. calcium, 0 mg. iron, 0 mg. vitamin C, 0 mg. beta-carotene
Makes 20 cookies

KITCHEN TIPS
When grinding the nuts in the food processor, be careful not to grind them too long, or they will turn into a paste.

Most cookbooks recommend that meringues be baked only in clear, dry weather, but this recipe is not humidity-sensitive and should turn out fine anytime.

ORANGE-MARSALA FRUITS

1 small cantaloupe (about
1¾ pounds)

¾ cup orange juice

3 tablespoons dry Marsala wine
(optional)

1 tablespoon sugar

¼ teaspoon grated orange zest

2 medium peaches, pitted and
sliced

2 medium nectarines, pitted and
sliced

¼ pound fresh or frozen sweet
cherries, halved and pitted

Mint leaves and strips of orange
zest, for garnish (optional)

An Englishman, John Woodhouse, is credited with the creation of Italy's most famous fortified wine. In the 18th century, hoping to produce a new beverage that would appeal to his countrymen, he applied the methods used to make Spanish and Portuguese fortified wines to the sweet white wines of Sicily. The result, named for the Sicilian city of Marsala, was (and is) an excellent cooking wine.

1 Halve the cantaloupe and remove the seeds. Using a melon baller, scoop the cantaloupe into balls or remove the rind and cut the cantaloupe into 1-inch pieces.

2 In large bowl, combine the orange juice, Marsala, if using, sugar and orange zest. Add the cantaloupe, peaches, nectarines and cherries, and stir to coat. Cover and refrigerate for 15 minutes, or longer if desired, to macerate the fruits.

3 To serve, spoon the fruits into a serving bowl or 4 dessert bowls or glasses. Garnish with mint leaves and strips of orange zest, if desired.

Preparation time 15 minutes • **Total time** 40 minutes • **Per serving** 148 calories, 0.9 g. fat (5% of calories), 0 g. saturated fat, 0 mg. cholesterol, 9 mg. sodium, 3.4 g. dietary fiber, 26 mg. calcium, 1 mg. iron, 70 mg. vitamin C, 2.5 mg. beta-carotene • **Serves 4**

Big, meaty Ox-Heart cherries add a luxurious note to this sophisticated dessert.

Red-blushed golden Queen Anne cherries are less common, but equally delicious.

CANNOLI

Shells

- ½ **cup all-purpose flour**
- ½ **cup sugar**
- 2 **tablespoons cornstarch**
- ½ **teaspoon ground cinnamon**
- 2 **tablespoons canola oil**
- 3 **large egg whites**
- 2 **tablespoons cold water**
- 1 **teaspoon vanilla extract**

Filling

- 1 **cup fat-free ricotta cheese**
- 1 **cup part-skim ricotta cheese**
- ½ **cup confectioners' sugar**
- 1 **teaspoon vanilla extract**
- 1 **teaspoon grated orange zest**
- 1 **tablespoon plus 1 teaspoon semisweet chocolate mini morsels, finely chopped**

Confectioners' sugar, for topping (optional)

Cannoli molds are sold at specialty cookware shops and through mail-order catalogues specializing in cookware.

To shape the shells, you can use small (½-inch diameter) cannoli molds, available at baking-supply shops; you could also form the shells around the handles of small whisks.

1 Preheat the oven to 400°. Spray 2 baking sheets with no-stick spray.

2 To make the shells, in a large bowl, combine the flour, sugar, cornstarch and cinnamon. In a small bowl, whisk together the oil, egg whites, water and vanilla. Make a well in the center of the dry ingredients, pour in the oil mixture and beat just until combined.

3 Working in two batches of 8 cannoli shells (4 per baking sheet), make 16 shells. To make a shell, spoon 1 tablespoon of the batter onto a baking sheet and smooth to a 4-inch circle. Leaving 3 inches between batter circles, repeat this 3 more times per baking sheet.

4 Bake one sheet of cannoli shells for 6 to 7 minutes, or until lightly browned at the edges and set. Remove from the oven and immediately place the second baking sheet in the oven. Remove a baked shell from the first sheet and shape it into a tube by curling it over a cannoli mold or whisk handle; repeat using as many molds as you have. When the shells have cooled on the molds and are crisp, gently slide them off. Repeat for the remaining baked shells. Respray the baking sheets with no-stick spray and repeat with the remaining batter.

5 To make the filling, place a sieve or fine-mesh strainer over a large bowl. Press the fat-free and part-skim ricotta cheeses through the seive or strainer to remove graininess. Add the confectioners' sugar, vanilla and orange zest to the cheeses, and stir until well combined. Stir in the chocolate morsels. Cover and refrigerate until ready to serve.

6 Just before serving, spoon the ricotta mixture into a pastry bag fitted with a large plain tip. Pipe the ricotta filling into the cannoli shells from both ends. Sprinkle with confectoners' sugar, if desired.

Preparation time 10 minutes • **Total time** 1 hour 10 minutes plus chilling time
Per serving 116 calories, 3.3 g. fat (26% of calories), 1 g. saturated fat,
5 mg. cholesterol, 47 mg. sodium, 0.1 g. dietary fiber, 119 mg. calcium, 0 mg. iron,
0 mg. vitamin C, 0.1 mg. beta-carotene • **Makes 16 cannoli**

INDEX

❧ ❧ ❧